bild

Physical interventions

A Policy Framework

A guide to the use of restrictive physical interventions with adults and children with learning disability and/or autism

Prepared by:

John Harris

Marion Cornick

Alan Jefferson

Richard Mills

Second edition

British Library Cataloguing in Publication Data

A CIP record for this book is available from the
Public Library

© BILD Publications 1996, 2008
Second edition 2008

BILD Publications is the imprint of:
British Institute of Learning Disabilities
Campion House
Green Street
Kidderminster
Worcestershire DY10 1JL

Telephone: 01562 723010
Fax: 01562 723029
E-mail: enquiries@bild.org.uk

Website: www.bild.org.uk

ISBN 978 1 905218 04 2

Printed in the UK by Latimer Trend & Company Ltd, Plymouth

BILD publications are distributed by:
BookSource
50 Cambuslang Road
Cambuslang
Glasgow G32 8NB

Telephone: 0845 370 0067
Fax: 0845 370 0068

For a publications catalogue with details of all
BILD books and journals telephone 01562 723010,
e-mail enquiries@bild.org.uk or visit the BILD
website www.bild.org.uk

'When I was 17, I was put in an adult psychiatric hospital. I tried to run away. But they brought me back. I was frightened because of the other patients. The staff restrained me and it hurt. They used to bend my thumb in and press your hand to hurt you. If you said anything they did it more and put your hand up your back. It was very intimidating... wrong... it made me even more stressed. I was a 5 foot 2 inch teenager. I didn't have a history of violence. They restrained me and hurt me. They just liked to use their power.'

Tee Randall, a woman with high-functioning autism

WILLIS: Sit him down, sit him down. If the King refuses food, he will be restrained. If he claims to have no appetite, he will be restrained. If he swears and indulges in meaningless discourse, he will be restrained. If he throws off his bedclothes, tears away his bandages, scratches at his sores, and if he does not strive every day and always towards his own recovery, then he must be restrained.

The King has been buckled into the chair and is helpless, a pathetic parody of the King on his throne.

KING: I am the King of England.
WILLIS: No, sir. You are the patient.

From *The Madness of King George* by Alan Bennett

Acknowledgements

We are grateful to David Allen for his contribution to the first edition.

The extract from *The Madness of King George* is reproduced by kind permission of the publisher Faber and Faber and the author Alan Bennett.

We are grateful to Tee Randall for permission to include her quotation.

Contents

Preface to the second edition

It is now over ten years since the first edition of *Physical Interventions: A Policy Framework* first appeared. The book has stood the test of time well. This could be interpreted as a tribute to the quality of the original material or, as seems more likely, a reflection of the slow and often stuttering progress we have made in helping people with severely challenging behaviour to lead ordinary lives. In many ways the continuing high level of interest in reactive approaches to managing challenging behaviour is disappointing because it suggests that preventative approaches are still not being used with sufficient frequency and consistency to obviate the need for potentially aversive techniques including physical interventions. Of even greater concern are the continuing revelations of ad hoc methods of physical intervention being employed by untrained and poorly supervised staff (the *Guardian*, 17 January 2007; *Community Care*, 15–21 February and 1–7 March 2007).

It is clear that the development and implementation of effective policies on the use of restrictive physical interventions is still unfinished business for many services. We acknowledge that this opportunity to revise and update the original text, while welcome in many ways, would not have been necessary had the ambition that inspired the first edition been realised.

Among the most surprising and gratifying responses to the first edition was the amount of interest shown by colleagues working outside the fields of autism and learning disability. Given that the last decade has witnessed some remarkable developments affecting the lives of those most frequently identified as presenting challenging behaviours – people with autism and/or a learning disability; young people with social, emotional and behavioural difficulties; and children and adults with mental illness – it seems unlikely that this second edition will be treated in the same way. Schools, local education authorities and children's trusts are now required to produce behaviour management policies that specifically address the use of restrictive physical interventions. NHS staff working with people with mental illness are required to have training on the use of physical interventions and the Commission for Social Care Inspection now routinely takes into account during inspections the use of restrictive physical interventions.

We have resisted the temptation to produce a policy framework that applies to all these different agencies and service user groups. Instead, we continue to focus on the needs of adults and children with learning disabilities and/or autism, while recognising that in practice this core group melds into other diagnostic or administrative categories. Learning disability and autism define our own sphere of competence and provide the surest ground for our efforts to revise and update policy and practice in respect of physical interventions.

Initially, the Department of Health, which funded the work leading up to the original publication (*Physical Interventions: A Policy Framework*, 1996), seemed content to see the potentially controversial topic of physical intervention being addressed at arm's length. BILD was successful in obtaining further funding for discrete projects on physical interventions, but it was not until the BBC broadcast two programmes showing staff physically abusing people with learning disabilities in residential homes in Kent (*McIntyre Undercover*, 1999) that the government decided to act. The timing turned out to be fortuitous, for the Department for Education and Skills had also launched a consultation on physical interventions in respect of pupils with special educational needs. With both departments looking to BILD for advice, a joint DH/DfES policy on physical interventions was not only logical but achievable (*Guidance on the Use of Restrictive Physical Interventions*, 2002). This is described in more detail in Chapter 2.

Other important developments were the publication of *BILD Code of Practice for Trainers in the Use of Physical Interventions* (BILD, 2001) that set rigorous standards for those involved in training staff in the safe use of restrictive physical interventions and the introduction of the voluntary Physical Interventions Accreditation Scheme by BILD in 2002 that enables anyone commissioning training to easily identify reputable providers.

Since 1996, governments in all four UK countries have sought to improve the provision of services for people with a learning disability by publishing high-profile policy statements. In England, the White Paper *Valuing People* recognised the importance of developing good practice in the use of restrictive physical interventions and referred to both *Physical Interventions: A Policy Framework* and the joint DH/DfES guidance although, paradoxically, this also served to highlight the dearth of other policy initiatives or incentives for improved practice to address the needs of adults and children who present severely challenging behaviours. Similarly, in Scotland a policy review commissioned by the Scottish Executive resulted in the publication of *The Same as You* and in Wales the Learning Disability Advisory Group produced a national plan for learning disability services called *Fulfilling the Promises*. Unsurprisingly, in Northern Ireland progress towards power sharing between unionist and nationalist politicians during this period precluded similar developments, although good practice in the use of restrictive physical interventions has been under discussion by commissioners and service providers.

One of the most widely welcomed contributions of the reviews conducted in England, Scotland and Wales was their forthright commitment to underpinning values, designed to provide common points of reference across all types of service provision. For example, *Valuing People* identified four core principles: rights, independence, choice and inclusion. Chapter 3 has been revised and updated to show how these values apply to the use of restrictive physical interventions.

Another important development during the last ten years has been the widespread acceptance of 'person-centred' approaches to service development, particularly in relation to accommodation where supported living is now the preferred model for all but the most severely disabled. The benefits of supported living are that services are provided in response to a person's choices about their preferred lifestyle, their aspirations for the future and how their needs can best be met. Rather than shoehorning people into predetermined services that in the past were often unimaginative and constraining, supported living seeks to liberate service users and enable them to take control of their own lives. To this extent, supported living approaches are entirely consistent with the values described in Chapter 3.

While endorsing the principles of supported living, we would emphasise that people who present challenging behaviours need a great deal of help if they are to take full advantage of the choices available to them. They are likely to need an array of very carefully planned supports from highly trained staff to help them adjust to, and benefit from, the new experiences associated with supported living environments. If these supports are not put in place, supported living may not only fail to deliver improvements in a person's quality of life, but may increase the likelihood of restrictive physical interventions being used to manage challenging behaviours. Chapters 8 and 9 remind managers and employers of their responsibilities for establishing effective policies on the use of restrictive physical interventions in different settings, including residential accommodation.

More recently, a re-examination of the legislation affecting people who are deemed not to have the mental capacity for making certain decisions (Mental Capacity Act 2005) has added further weight to the argument that every effort should be made to involve service users in deciding whether physical interventions should be used to help manage their behaviour and, if so, what type of procedure or 'holding technique' is most likely to be successful. There is now scope for service users (or their representatives) to make a legal challenge if professionals or paid staff do not demonstrate due process in coming to a decision or if they fail to listen to their views when making significant decisions about their lives and the treatments available to them.

Recent improvements in procedures for safeguarding children (*Safeguarding Children*, 2005) and adults (*No Secrets*, 2001) have made it possible to integrate policies on the use of restrictive physical interventions with arrangements to promote information sharing and co-ordinated action in response to concerns about abuse and neglect. Those responsible for good practice in the use of restrictive physical interventions should make contact with their respective local authority officers responsible for promoting a partnership approach to safeguarding adults and children across statutory, voluntary and independent sector agencies.

While there was plenty of anecdotal evidence of the success of *Physical Interventions* it was not until the publication of a research evaluation by Professor Murphy at the University of Kent that we could be sure of its impact (Murphy, Kelly-Pike, McGill, Jones and Byatt, 2003). The research looked at the development of policies for managing challenging behaviour in statutory and voluntary sector agencies for people with learning disabilities. The authors concluded that the majority of participants in the study were 'overwhelmingly positive' about the usefulness of this book in their day-to-day work.

One significant change that runs throughout this second edition concerns terminology. With hindsight we recognise that the term 'physical interventions' refers to a broader class of actions than those addressed in this book. For example, stroking, hugging and providing physical support are all examples of physical intervention. Following our earlier statement that physical intervention is best defined in terms of some degree of physical force to limit or restrict movement or mobility, we employ the preferred DH/DfES term – restrictive physical intervention – throughout this revised edition.

While a more precise definition helps to clarify the specific area of practice this book seeks to address, it does not necessarily follow that all service users will respond to different kinds of physical intervention in similar ways. For example, some service users have told us that their preference is to be held very firmly (ie for a restrictive physical intervention to be employed) when they are distressed, while others have said that even a gentle touch, or stroke, intended to be reassuring, can provoke further anxiety. It is also clear that for some people the calming effect of restrictive physical intervention is so great that they will actively seek it from others or indeed find ways to impose it on themselves (Harris, 1996). This variability in the response of different people to any kind of physical intervention highlights the importance of creating intervention plans that reflect, as far as possible, individual preferences, whether openly stated or inferred from observation over a period of time. (Notwithstanding these differences, the term 'restraint' is still current and is even employed in recent government documents that espouse the principles set out in this book. For example, see the section on Scottish law in Chapter 2 and the English Care Homes Regulations 2001.)

Chapter 1
Introduction

Responding to challenging behaviours

Developing services to help people with a learning disability live ordinary lives remains a formidable and complex task. It is, perhaps, the area that has benefited least from *Valuing People* and its associated implementation strategy. Commissioning high-quality local services for vulnerable people with severe and complex disabilities requires courage, considerable expertise and commitment, both in terms of policy objectives and ongoing costs, over the long term. People who behave in ways that are considered dangerous, socially inappropriate or disruptive make special demands on services. They present us with the challenge of responding to their needs and helping them to lead valued lives in spite of their problematic behaviours (Blunden and Allen, 1987).

Some challenging behaviours raise special concerns for services because they significantly increase the risk of injury to the person concerned or to other people. Examples of these behaviours are violence towards other people, self-injury and actions performed with a reckless disregard for safety, such as wandering across a busy road. When repeatedly confronted with these behaviours, services may decide that they have no alternative other than to restrict the person's range of movements by force. This is often referred to as a 'physical restraint', although in this book the term 'restrictive physical intervention' will be used. There is no national or regional approach to documenting the use of restrictive physical interventions, but from service-based audits, research, recent investigations and reports by the Commission for Social Care Inspection and the Health Care Commission we know that they are widely employed in services for people with a learning disability and/or autism, especially in response to violent or aggressive behaviour.

The use of restrictive physical interventions in response to challenging behaviours is problematic for a number of reasons:

- Using force to overpower a person who is violent or aggressive may result in injuries to staff and service users (Hill and Spreat, 1987).

- The use of unplanned restrictive physical interventions is likely to be associated with high levels of psychological stress for both staff and service users.

- In many situations the use of force will be unlawful (Lyon and Pimor, 2004).

- The unregulated use of restrictive physical interventions can lead to abuse (persons who present challenging behaviour are at greater risk of abuse by carers even when restrictive physical interventions are not employed).

- The use of restrictive physical interventions may not be in the best interest of the service user.

- Restrictive physical interventions may be used in situations where other non-physical methods would be more effective.

- Inappropriate use of restrictive physical interventions may lead to an escalation in challenging behaviours.

- The use of restrictive physical interventions may conflict with key service values such as respect, dignity and choice for service users.

- The use of restrictive physical interventions with people with atypical sensory sensitivities may result in either unreasonable levels of pain for those with a low pain threshold or, for people with high pain thresholds, increased risk of injury.

Notwithstanding these drawbacks, the behavioural challenges presented by a small number of service users mean that some form of restrictive physical intervention may be unavoidable. Faced with such circumstances, many services have developed policies that set out permissible forms of restrictive physical intervention and safeguards to protect service users and staff.

Clear guidance regarding the legal responsibilities of service providers and the legal protection available to service users is an essential prerequisite for the development of good practice in relation to restrictive physical interventions. Chapter 2 is a completely revised and updated summary of the law as it relates to restrictive physical interventions. Those seeking more detailed advice on legal issues are referred to Lyon and Pimor (2004).

The next step for service managers and their staff is to determine, within the parameters established by law, what steps they can take to manage the person's challenging behaviour, including the extent to which restrictive physical interventions may be justified. A key reference is the comprehensive joint guidance issued by the Department of Health and the Department for Education and Skills (2002).

Insofar as the first edition of this book provided the basis for the development of the joint guidance (Harris, 2004), it adheres to the same underlying principles and seeks the same practical outcomes. The main advantage of this text is that with a great deal more space it is possible to set out in some detail the way in which common principles can be applied in practice.

The ideas presented here are based on a consultation exercise carried out by BILD in collaboration with provider organisations throughout the UK who were invited to submit examples of policy statements on the use of restrictive physical interventions or restraint. Not surprisingly, organisations differed considerably regarding the content, the length and the details they provided in their policy documents. It seems likely that this variability reflected local circumstances and experiences. It also underlined the complexity of the many, and often conflicting, considerations that need to be addressed by a policy statement on the use of restrictive physical interventions. The materials that were submitted were carefully reviewed and many of the issues raised are explored in the following pages.

It should be emphasised that this book is not intended as an 'off-the-peg' policy that can be implemented wholesale and unchanged in any service setting; rather, it provides an overview of the many issues that need to be considered by any organisation seeking to develop a policy on restrictive physical interventions. Readers are invited to work through the whole book before deciding how the issues raised in each chapter relate to their own service.

Restrictive physical interventions

The following pages set out a framework to help organisations working with adults and children with learning disabilities and/or autism to develop clear and effective policies on the use of restrictive physical intervention procedures. While the term 'restraint' is still widely used, in recent years 'physical intervention' or 'restrictive physical intervention' has become associated in the UK with a particular approach or style of working with people who are violent or aggressive. Whereas 'restraint' methods are concerned with establishing compliance by using force, restrictive physical interventions are one part of a wider strategy in which varying degrees of force may be used as a last resort. While restraint suggests that the primary objective is to exercise control over the person being restrained, restrictive physical interventions are deployed with the aim of minimising the use of force and restoring self-control to the person concerned as soon as possible. These different objectives in turn suggest very different ways of working in practice.

There are three broad categories of restrictive physical intervention:

1. **Direct physical contact between a member of staff and a service user**

   Examples include:

   - using manual guidance to prevent someone wandering into a busy main road
   - holding a person's hand to stop stereotyped movements
   - holding a person's arms and legs to prevent them from attacking someone

2. **The use of barriers, such as locked doors, to limit freedom of movement**

   Examples include:

   - placing a child in a chair with a desk in front so that they cannot easily stand up or move away
   - placing door catches or bolts beyond the reach of service users
   - locking doors

3. **Materials or equipment that restrict or prevent movement**

   Examples include:

   - strapping someone into a wheelchair
   - tucking sheets into a bed so that movement is restricted
   - placing splints on a person's arms to restrict their movement

Why do service providers need a policy on restrictive physical interventions?

Policies that help to regulate the use of restrictive physical intervention are necessary for a number of reasons:

- Adults and children with learning disabilities and/or autism often present challenging behaviours; restrictive physical interventions may be seen as a necessary or indeed an inevitable response by staff.

- Adults and children with learning disabilities and/or autism are extremely vulnerable and are often not able to protect themselves from abusive practices, including the misuse of restrictive physical interventions.

- Restrictive physical interventions that are misused are likely to cause pain, physical injury and psychological distress.

- Without an effective policy it can be difficult to maintain a distinction between using restrictive physical interventions as part of a carefully planned response to challenging behaviours and using it as a punishment.

- In some circumstances the use, or threatened use, of a restrictive physical intervention is unlawful.

- On the rare occasions where restrictive physical interventions are justified, they should only be used in the best interests of the service user.

- Staff often feel threatened, anxious or frightened by challenging behaviours; developing an effective policy is therefore part of an employer's responsibility towards their staff.

- A policy statement makes explicit the safeguards that must be in place before a restrictive physical intervention is used; it affords protection to the service user, to staff and to the organisation.

This policy document is designed to help all organisations that provide services for children and adults with learning disabilities and/or autism. (In the subsequent pages the terms 'people' and 'service user' refer to children and adults with a learning disability and/or autism.) Most organisations will use it as a framework for developing policies that suit their own particular circumstances. In order to do this, it is important to be clear about what a policy is and how it helps to regulate good practice.

What is a policy?

A policy is a set of general statements that help individuals (eg members of staff who work directly with service users) to make sound judgements and take appropriate actions. In general terms, sound decisions and appropriate actions are those that are legal, consistent with the aims and values of the organisation and in the best interests of the people they serve. An effective policy is, therefore, central to the process of setting, monitoring and raising service standards.

Policy, procedures and guidelines for practice

A policy is designed to establish the broad parameters within which service systems operate. All aspects of a service should be consistent with the policy statements. Some aspects of a service will require more specific delineation, for example where there is a high level of risk or where the service depends upon close liaison between different members of staff. In these circumstances, a standard procedure may be established. Procedures specify the minimum acceptable standards of practice.

Guidelines for practice indicate what staff need to do or to know in order to comply with specific procedures. Figure 1 provides a summary of the relationship between policy, procedure and guidelines of practice.

Figure 1

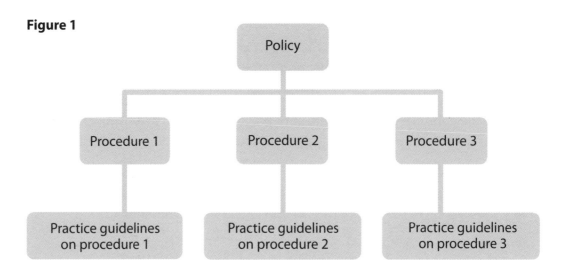

A policy on restrictive physical intervention should establish the general principles by which staff can decide whether or not, and under what precise circumstances, it is permissible and appropriate to use a restrictive physical intervention with a particular adult or child. The policy will need to explain the law as it relates to restrictive physical interventions, the aims and values of the organisation and what is meant by the best interests of the service user. It should also indicate how the organisation ensures that the policy is implemented in practice. Each of these areas is explored in more detail in the chapters that follow.

How can a policy help develop better services?

A clear policy is only the first step towards establishing good practice. To be effective a policy must be implemented. This means developing related procedures and providing staff with guidelines that describe in more detail what they should and should not do in specific circumstances. It also involves training staff and monitoring performance to ensure that practice is consistent with the policy and associated guidelines.

No policy can adequately address every eventuality that is likely to occur in an organisation serving people with learning disabilities. For this reason, policies should be designed to help services improve their practice over time. This involves staff working together to plan and evaluate current practice and to develop new approaches. At some point the policy itself may need to be reviewed in the light of experience. Staff are more likely to initiate change and strive for improved practice if they are explicitly encouraged to take an active part in formulating and implementing the policy. The children and adults who use a service are more likely to respond positively to new ways of working if they are consulted and given opportunities to contribute to the development of the policy.

About this book

Who should read this book?

This book is designed to help all those who have an interest in or a responsibility for the provision of services to adults and children with a learning disability and/or autism. It will be of particular interest to:

1. **Children's services**

   - lead officers responsible for commissioning
   - managers of residential and short-term break services
   - head teachers in schools
   - care staff in residential services
   - teachers and learning support staff
   - school governors
   - local education authorities
   - inspectors and regulators
   - parents

2. **Services for adults**

   - lead officers responsible for commissioning
   - managers of residential and short-term break services
   - managers of community and domiciliary services
   - care staff in day and residential services
   - staff working for NHS trusts
   - regulatory staff in the Commission for Social Care Inspection and the Healthcare Commission
   - parents and other family members
   - advocates

The establishment of good practice around the use of a controversial procedure such as restrictive physical intervention will require close collaboration and a concerted effort on the part of all those who have a stake in the provision of high-quality services. This book is recognised as a key resource to assist those seeking to improve the way in which restrictive physical interventions are employed with people with learning disabilities.

How to use this book

The material in the following chapters has been set out so that it can be easily read and understood. There are no short cuts to the development of good practice and those who consult this book are urged to read all of it. There are nine chapters that deal briefly with key topic areas. Throughout the book you will find highlighted information:

- **Key policy principles** that may be used to develop organisational policies on the use of restrictive physical interventions, numbered consecutively and summarised in Appendix 1 at the end of the book

- **Checklists** to assist implementation

- **Good practice** and **Poor practice** examples

- **Agenda for action** lists that set out the main points in the form of questions for services and that are summarised in Appendix 2 at the end of the book. These questions are intended to help service providers evaluate and improve their use of restrictive physical interventions. They should also help commissioners to determine how competently different provider organisations manage the use of restrictive physical interventions. They should also help service users, their families and advocates find out how successfully each service has planned its use of restrictive physical interventions for individual service users.

Terminology

The practical value of a policy will depend on its clarity and precision. It is important that the words used are clearly understood and free from ambiguity. At this point it is helpful to make explicit reference to a number of key terms:

Learning disability is used throughout for the sake of consistency. Many people working with children will be more familiar with the term 'learning difficulty'. The 1993 Education Act defines learning difficulty as 'a condition that exists if a child has a greater difficulty in learning than the majority of children of his age or a disability which either prevents or hinders him from making use of educational facilities of a kind generally provided for children of his age in schools within the area of the local education authority'. The term 'learning disability' is usually employed when describing adults. Learning disability is a permanent condition arising during childhood or adolescence that is characterised by a state of arrested or incomplete development of mind that includes significant impairment of intelligence and social functioning. In this book the term 'learning disability' is used to refer to both children (with a learning difficulty) and adults (with a learning disability).

Autism is a term used to describe a spectrum of conditions that arises during infancy or childhood, which are characterised by impaired social interaction, delayed or deviant language development, and a preference for sameness as shown by stereotyped play patterns, abnormal preoccupations or resistance to change. Autism often occurs in association with learning disability, but can also be present without any additional intellectual impairment. In addition, many autistic individuals present with complex sensory impairments, including hypersensitivity or hyposensitivity to touch or pain, which has a particular relevance for restrictive physical interventions.

Challenging behaviour refers to 'culturally abnormal behaviour of such intensity, frequency or duration that the physical safety of the person or others is likely to be placed in serious jeopardy, or behaviour that is likely to seriously limit the use of, or result in the person being denied access to, ordinary community facilities' (Emerson, 1995). In service settings, it is primarily behaviours that are associated with increased risk of injury to the person concerned, or to others, that are most frequently managed with a restrictive physical intervention. These include:

- **Violence** that is directed toward other people (Emerson, Barrett, Bell et al, 1987; Harris and Russell, 1989; Emerson, 1995) and violence that is less clearly targeted and arises from distress, confusion or panic are often managed with a restrictive physical intervention.

- **Self-directed violence** or **self-injury** is another relatively common form of challenging behaviour associated with the use of restrictive physical interventions. Examples include hitting the head with a clenched fist, banging the head against hard objects, skin picking and eye gouging.

- **Behaving with a reckless disregard for their own safety or for the safety of others**, (eg by wandering across busy roads or persistently setting fires) may result in people being subjected to a restrictive physical intervention.

- **Behaviour that causes serious damage to property** may, in some settings, be managed using restrictive physical interventions. Whether or not the use of restrictive physical interventions is an appropriate way to respond to these behaviours can only be decided after a careful examination of the circumstances surrounding individual cases.

Physical restraint is a term that has, over time, acquired a number of negative connotations. It is also a term that is closely linked with a particular kind of approach to the management of aggressive and violent behaviour – 'control and restraint' or 'C and R'. For these reasons, throughout this book the more neutral term 'restrictive physical intervention' has been used.

Restrictive physical intervention refers to the actions by which one person restricts the movements of another. Examples include holding another person by the arm, tying someone to a bed or chair, using a splint to limit the movement of an arm or leg and locking a door so that an adult or child cannot leave a room. Restrictive physical intervention involves limiting a person's freedom of movement and *continuing to do so against resistance*. It is, therefore, qualitatively different from other forms of physical contact such as manual prompting, physical guidance or support that might be used in teaching or therapy.

In some settings a skilled teacher or therapist may use a blend of prompts, physical guidance and, for very short periods of time, restrictive physical intervention, to assist a person in completing an exercise or learning a skill. However, in such circumstances, if restrictive physical interventions were to be sustained against resistance over a period of more than a few seconds, the fundamental character of the activity would have changed from 'therapy' or 'teaching' to one of 'managing challenging behaviour'. Urgent consideration would need to be given to the sequence of events leading up the challenging behaviour and it is unlikely that repeated use of a restrictive physical intervention would be considered the most appropriate response. Because restrictive physical interventions are intrusive, often distressing, and potentially harmful, they should always be considered a 'last resort' response to challenging behaviour, to be employed only after other approaches have been fully explored.

It is helpful to distinguish between **emergency interventions** or **unplanned interventions** that are used on the spur of the moment without previous preparation or discussion, and **planned interventions** that implement agreed procedures in response to anticipated incidents and clearly defined behaviours. While there may be rare occasions on which emergency interventions are appropriate, the emphasis in this book is upon preparation and planning to ensure that, as far as possible, restrictive physical interventions are always used in the best interests of the service user.

People who use services or the shorthand 'service user' refers to children and adults with different degrees of learning disability and/or autism and is used in preference to 'client'. There is no generic term to describe people with learning disabilities that is completely satisfactory.

What should be included in a policy on restrictive physical interventions?

There are a number of fundamental questions that any service should consider in relation to the use of restrictive physical interventions. These are summarised in the checklist below and elaborated in the following chapters.

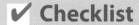 **Checklist**

A policy on restrictive physical interventions

1. What are the legal responsibilities of a service provider and what legal protection is afforded service users who present challenging behaviours?

2. What are the values and the ethical standards of the service against which any decision to use or not to use restrictive physical interventions can be judged?

3. How can the use of restrictive physical interventions be minimised through preventative strategies and alternative approaches?

4. What steps can be taken to ensure that restrictive physical interventions are always used in the best interests of service users?

continued

5   What risks are involved for service users, staff and members of the public when using restrictive physical interventions and how can these be minimised?

6   How can restrictive physical interventions be used without compromising the safety or the well-being of service users?

7   What can service managers do to ensure that policies are properly implemented?

8   What responsibilities do employers and managers have towards staff?

9   How can staff training assist in the development of good practice?

Chapter 2

The law and restrictive physical interventions

Introduction

People with learning disabilities and severe challenging behaviour are entitled to the same level of legal protection as other citizens. Any restrictive physical intervention by definition places a constraint on a person's liberty and must, therefore, always be legally as well as professionally justified. This chapter provides a broad overview of the law affecting the use of restrictive physical interventions. Without a good working knowledge of the legal framework, people working in settings where restrictive physical interventions are used could inadvertently break the law and/or compromise the integrity of their colleagues, managers and employers. This could leave them, or their employers, vulnerable to civil or criminal proceedings.

This is not an exhaustive or particularly detailed summary. On the contrary, its purpose is to set out in relatively simple terms the various aspects of the law that relate to the use of restrictive physical interventions. However, it is now significantly longer and covers more ground than the corresponding chapter in the first edition of this book. It makes reference to law enshrined in legislation and to that which derives from past cases – the common law – and also to the differences between civil and criminal law. Furthermore, in response to feedback on the first edition, additional sections have been introduced dealing with the law in Scotland and human rights law. Additional information on legislation, guidance and regulations is also included. Nevertheless, it should be emphasised that this chapter is not intended as a practice guide and does not include any illustrative examples. Similarly, while it will provide readers with a legal background with a useful introduction, anyone seeking a comprehensive review of this topic is referred to *Physical Interventions and the Law* (Lyon and Pimor, 2004). This chapter relies heavily on Professor Lyon's work.

Inevitably, for practitioners the immediate concern is likely to be 'How do I do the right thing for this service user without breaking the law?' For example, is it permissible to hold someone who is hurting themself or perhaps is about to harm others? At the heart of this subject is the need to balance 'duty of care' – the responsibility of carers and service providers to act in the best interests of service users – with the detailed requirements of the legal framework. While this is not always easy to achieve, a basic understanding of the law will, we hope, enable practitioners to make these judgments with greater confidence.

The legal framework

The law is a complex system of rules that sets out the rights and responsibilities of individuals and organisations in a society and that generally reflects the current values and standards of that society. It is there to protect the freedom of individuals to go about their lives without interference or restrictions imposed by other people. Any limit on our freedom as citizens (eg using a seatbelt or not smoking in public places) must have legal backing.

Types of law

Civil law is concerned with the regulation of conduct between private individuals. If any person is aggrieved or injured by another person's conduct they may opt to take action in a civil court against the other person. The civil wrong that has been experienced is, in England, sometimes referred to as a 'tort', defined as 'a wrongful act or omission for which damages can be obtained in a civil court by the person wronged' (Martin, 2002). A successful action may result in the awarding of damages (monetary compensation) but other possible options include an injunction (an order of the court forbidding the wrongdoer from acting in a particular way or ordering them to perform a certain act) designed to ensure that the victim comes to no further harm.

Criminal law deals with conduct that society has deemed unacceptable and has made unlawful. The criminal law is made up of a series of offences that are set out either in statutes made by Parliament or in the 'common law' (see below). Prosecution in a criminal law matter is not undertaken by a private individual but is conducted, on behalf of the police, by the Crown Prosecution Service in England and Wales, the Public Prosecution Service in Northern Ireland and by the Procurator Fiscal in Scotland. If the offender is found guilty the sentencing options can include imprisonment, a compensation order, a fine or a community rehabilitation or punishment order.

Human rights law provides an overarching structure that enables individuals' rights (as set out in the European Convention on Human Rights) to be protected through actions in national courts. Action can only be brought against the State or public bodies and not against private individuals. However, the courts have a general obligation to interpret the law in accordance with the Convention so the rights contained in it must also be taken into account in any action involving private individuals.

Employment law relates to workplace safety and to the conduct and activities of everyone within the workplace, be they employers or employees. Employment law is relevant in relation to the legal responsibilities of employers for the safety and welfare of their staff and service users or customers. Restrictive physical interventions may be justified as a means of keeping staff safe, but employers must also consider the consequences for service users and other people in the work environment.

The use of restrictive physical interventions needs to be considered from all these perspectives. Any inappropriate use of restrictive physical interventions could result in action under both criminal and civil law.

Sources of the law

Statute law (legislation) is created and reformed by Parliament. Acts of Parliament create specific rights and legal duties and individuals' day-to-day activities must be consistent with these statutory requirements. Legislation has to be agreed by both Houses of Parliament and signed by the Queen before it becomes law. Numerous Acts of Parliament have implications for the use of restrictive physical interventions.

Common law (sometimes known as case law) encompasses decisions made by courts, often over hundreds of years, in particular cases that amplify and clarify the meaning of statutes and create 'precedents' that must usually be followed when making judgements on similar cases in the future. Since it includes a huge number of individual judgements, common law is extremely complex and is constantly being modified and updated. For this reason, the development of an informed overview requires detailed research by an experienced lawyer. If there is a conflict between common law and statute law, the latter takes precedence.

Secondary (or delegated) legislation arises from provisions contained within statute law that grant to the relevant Secretary of State powers to make Rules or Regulations that provide greater detail about the provisions in the statute. An example is the Care Homes Regulations 2001, made using powers contained in the Care Standards Act 2000. Regulations have to be brought to the attention of Parliament (the technical term is 'laid before Parliament') and this provides MPs who are concerned about their content with an opportunity to ask for a vote to take place before they are implemented. If no vote is requested the Regulations come into effect without any additional action. Regulations are 'law' just as primary statutes are.

Guidance and circulars may also be issued by the relevant Secretary of State or by one of the devolved UK government bodies such as the Welsh Assembly Government or the Scottish Executive. Guidance is not law and is, therefore, not mandatory but, as a general principle, should be followed unless there are very good reasons for not doing so. Guidance to English local authorities issued under the provisions of Section 7 of the Local Authority Social Services Act 1970 is strongly binding on social services authorities. An example is the *Guidance for Restrictive Physical Interventions* issued jointly by the Department of Health and the Department for Education and Skills in 2002.

Legislation and case law in Scotland and Northern Ireland is different from in England and Wales. While much of this book is relevant to all parts of the UK, anyone working in Scotland or Northern Ireland is advised to familiarise themselves with the specifics of the legislation that applies there.

Duty of care

A duty of care exists when one person (or a group of people) is presumed to have responsibility for another person (or group of people), for example a teacher in relation to a class of children, or a nurse in relation to his or her patients. In these and similar circumstances duties and responsibilities are imposed on professionals or paid carers (Ashton and Ward, 1992). In general terms this requires them to take reasonable care to avoid acts or omissions that are likely to cause harm to another person. Judgements about what is 'reasonable' are often not clear-cut, but the following factors are relevant:

- the conduct of practitioners in similar settings with similar skills and responsibilities

- relevant expert opinion

- the range of available alternatives

- the foreseeable risks associated with a course of action

When there is an incident of challenging behaviour the first aim of any carer should be to try to ensure that the service user, and anyone else affected by the violence, does not sustain harm. If this is not possible, the secondary aim should be to reduce the level of harm as much as possible.

The law in England and Wales

Key offences or torts

Under law, every citizen is entitled to live without interference from others. Three main forms of interference are to be found in both criminal and civil law. Generally, the criminal law provides a narrower specification for 'interference' than the equivalent civil law.

False imprisonment is defined in criminal law as 'the unlawful and intentional or reckless restraint of a person's freedom of movement from a particular place'. In civil law false imprisonment occurs when a person intentionally or directly restrains another's freedom of movement. Lyon (1994) offers a number of examples of things that could be regarded as false imprisonment: seclusion; confinement in a room; tying someone to a chair; and preventing (by any means) a person from leaving a room or building. Whether or not the person is aware of the restrictions that have been imposed is not relevant; locking the door of a bedroom in which someone is asleep can still constitute false imprisonment.

Assault has no statutory definition within the criminal law but is generally defined as 'any act – and not a mere omission to act – by which a person intentionally or recklessly causes another to apprehend immediate unlawful violence... The act must be accompanied by hostile intent' (Richardson et al, 2003). The act does not have to take place, but the victim must fear that it will take place. An assault can occur without actual physical contact with the victim. Actions like shaking a fist and using threatening words fall within the criminal definition. In civil law an assault is any act that directly and either intentionally or negligently causes the victim to fear that they will be subjected to immediate violence. Lyon (1994) offers a number of examples of things that may be regarded as assault: shaking a fist; throwing an object; drawing an injection; and the threatened use of a restraining device.

Battery is similar to assault, the main difference being that in criminal law the actual application of force to the victim (whether intended or reckless) must take place. Any unlawful physical contact, including the slightest touching, can amount to battery and there is no need to prove that harm or pain has been caused. Battery can occur even when the touching is not directly applied to the victim's physical body, for example by the grabbing of their clothes. In civil law, battery is defined as 'any act of the defendant which directly and either intentionally or negligently causes some physical contact with the plaintiff without the plaintiff's consent' (Brazier, 1993) (in this definition, the term 'plaintiff' is used in the same way as the term 'victim' is used elsewhere). Lyon (1994) gives examples of actions that may constitute battery: touching; holding; pushing; stitching up clothing; and putting to bed. The offence of battery will always include the offence of assault but the reverse is not necessarily the case.

Lyon's examples illustrate some of the actions that are covered by the criminal and civil law but they are not a complete or exhaustive list.

Other less common, but potentially relevant, criminal offences are contained in the Offences Against the Person Act 1861 and include: assault occasioning actual bodily harm; malicious wounding or inflicting grievous bodily harm; and wounding or causing grievous bodily harm with intent. More extreme still are the various homicide offences including manslaughter and murder.

Negligence, a civil law offence, may also apply. Negligence is a complex matter but basically involves failing to discharge a duty of care. Lyon and Pimor (2004) suggest that there are four main elements in the tort of negligence:

1. the defendant (ie the perpetrator of the act) owes a legal duty of care to the plaintiff

2. the defendant has breached this duty by falling below the standard of care demanded of them

3. the plaintiff has suffered damage as a result of the breach of duty

4. the damage suffered by the plaintiff was not too remote (ie the interval between the breach of duty and the damage suffered is not so long as to make the causal relationship seem implausible)

Defences

Reading the previous chapter could easily lead carers and service providers to form a view that all forms of physical intervention are illegal in all circumstances. Although the law is designed to protect people from unwarranted interference from others, it also recognises that there are occasions when such interference is not only reasonable but may be highly desirable. For example, it might be preferable for a person who is clearly intent upon committing suicide to be locked in a room under close supervision rather than be left to go ahead and commit suicide. The reasonableness of such an action would be based on whether the 'false imprisonment' is considered to have a less serious impact on the individual than the suicide attempt.

In criminal and civil law there are a number of recognised defences that may be used to 'justify' or 'excuse' an otherwise illegal act. Some are common to both including: consent; self-defence; necessity; and mistake, but it should be noted that there are differences in the way these defences can be applied in criminal and civil matters.

Consent Generally, when the victim has consented to the action being taken, no offence is deemed to have occurred.

Necessity There are situations where some action must be taken and it is a matter of choosing the course of action that would result in the least harm. Here the principle of 'best interest' is key.

Self-defence A proportionate amount of force may be taken by an individual to protect them from an attack or injury. However, the force must be commensurate with the action a reasonable person would take and must cease when the danger has disappeared.

Mistake If a person acts on the basis of a genuine misunderstanding of the facts of the circumstances this may be an acceptable defence.

Criminal law defences

Duress of circumstances An action may be justified if the person who takes it believes that without taking it there is a threat of serious injury or death. However, only the amount of force necessary to avoid the incident must be used.

Lawful correction In some circumstances, reasonable action to prevent an individual harming themself, others or property can be justified. However, defining 'reasonable force' is not easy, and views of what is acceptable can change over time. This defence cannot be used to justify immoderate or excessive chastisement or corporal punishment.

Common law and statutory power to detain the insane Although there is no specific common law power to apprehend or detain a person simply on the basis that they are suffering from a mental disorder, there may in some circumstances be justification for taking action, for example by the use of seclusion, to protect an individual who has severe learning disabilities and is presenting severe challenging behaviour.

Prevention of a breach of the peace or a crime This may be an acceptable defence where action is taken to deal with a person who is being either a threat to themself, or to the person taking the action or another person or is about to inflict damage to property or commit a crime involving some degree of force.

Civil law defences

Statutory authority Some statutes make provision for the lawful carrying out of acts that in other circumstances would be an offence. For example, the Mental Health Act 1983 contains provisions that permit patients to be lawfully detained in hospital.

Illegality Generally, if the victim suffers injury while committing an illegal act, damages cannot be claimed against the person who caused the injury. However, the amount of violence used must not be excessive in the circumstances.

Inevitable accident If injury is the result of an accident that is beyond the control of a carer they will not be held liable provided all reasonable precautions have been taken.

A common feature of many of these defences is that they are based on action that is judged to be 'reasonable' in the circumstances. This book contains guidance that, if followed, will assist carers and service providers to demonstrate that action taken in response to challenging behaviour is reasonable.

Some relevant legislation

There is no legislation that *specifically* addresses the issue of the use of restrictive physical interventions with adults and children. There are, however, a number of laws that have direct relevance to the subject. This chapter includes only a brief reference to the main legislation and again readers are encouraged to consult more comprehensive texts (such as Lyon and Pimor, 2004) for more detailed information.

Offences Against the Person Act 1861 This Act describes a number of offences, mainly different types of assault, that could legally compromise a carer who uses restrictive physical interventions with a service user.

Mental Health Act 1983 Though commonly associated with psychiatric illness this Act may, in some circumstances, apply to people with learning disabilities. It is concerned with the care and treatment of individuals and emphasises the need to balance protecting the rights of individuals with protecting the well-being of the whole community. It allows for the detention of individuals in carefully prescribed circumstances. However, Section 127(2) of the Act makes it an offence for an individual to ill-treat or wilfully neglect a mentally disordered person who falls within the remit of the Act, and this provision could form the basis of a challenge to any person who uses restrictive physical interventions inappropriately in such circumstances.

Children Act 1989 This Act contains a number of provisions to safeguard and promote the welfare of children. One of the most important of these provisions instructs courts that when they are making decisions about a child their most important consideration, the one that overrides all others, must be the child's welfare. This is sometimes referred to as the 'paramountcy principle'. Lyon (1994) argues that although the law does not specifically require it, it follows that 'when seeking to provide for the care, control and safety of children with learning disabilities who also present severe challenging behaviour... parents, carers and professionals must always consider whether their actions are being performed in the paramount interests of the child'. The Children Act 1989 contains a 'welfare checklist' that sets out issues that courts must take account of when making decisions about children. The checklist provides a valuable framework against which carers and service providers can test decisions about the care of children (and to some extent adults) with learning disabilities and severe challenging behaviour.

Care Standards Act 2000 and its associated Regulations These provide the framework within which residential and domiciliary care services for adults and children are regulated. The overall purpose of the legislation is to foster and promote high-quality care services and give service users a good quality of life. The Regulations make specific reference to the use of restrictive physical interventions.

- Regulation 13 (7) of the Care Homes Regulations 2001 says *'the registered person shall ensure that no service user is subject to physical restraint unless restraint of the kind employed is the only practicable means of securing the welfare of that or any other service user and there are exceptional circumstances'.*

- Regulation 13 (8) of the Care Homes Regulations 2001 says *'on any occasion on which a service user is subject to physical restraint, the registered person shall record the circumstances, including the nature of the restraint'.*

- Regulations 14 (10) and (11) of the Domiciliary Care Agencies Regulations 2002 contains the same or similar wording. (The care provided for people living in supported accommodation is, of course, often provided by domiciliary care agencies.)

- Regulation 17 of the Children's Homes Regulations 2001 also contains similar, but much more detailed requirements about permissible ways of managing children's behaviour.

Human Rights Act 1998 This Act is the means by which the European Convention of Human Rights is made operational in the UK. A number of provisions are relevant to the use of restrictive physical interventions:

- Article 2 states that everyone has the right to life and that this right ought to be protected by law.

- Article 3 prohibits torture and inhuman or degrading treatment or punishment.

- Article 5 acknowledges that everyone has a right to liberty and that it should only be restricted if there is a specific legal justification.

- Article 8 says that everyone has a right to have their private and family life respected.

- Article 10 covers people's right to hold opinions and receive and communicate information and ideas.

- Article 14 outlaws discrimination of all types.

- Article 17 says that no state, group or person has the right to engage in activities designed to restrict the rights set out in the European Convention.

It has already been pointed out that legal actions using the provisions of the Human Rights Act 1998 are only possible against public authorities. At the time of writing, a recent judgement concerning the Leonard Cheshire Foundation has stated that independent sector organisations, such as national charities, are not public authorities. This gives service users in care services operated by such organisations a different level of protection than that enjoyed by people who live in council-run services. Nevertheless, the principles of the Act remain generally applicable to decisions about what actions are reasonable, regardless of the type of service provider.

Employment law is complex and covers a wide range of statutes. It is relevant in so far as employers may sanction the use of restrictive physical interventions in order to maintain the health, safety and welfare of themselves, their employees and people who make use of services. Employers have to ensure: that all members of staff are competent (this requirement is relevant to the provision of training in the use of restrictive physical interventions covered in Chapter 10); that the workplace is safe; that proper plant and equipment is provided and that systems of work are safe (this being particularly relevant to ensuring that policies and procedures for the use of restrictive physical interventions are fit for purpose). Relevant legislation includes: the Health and Safety at Work Act 1974 and its associated Regulations (the Management of Health and Safety at Work Regulations 1999 and the Manual Handling Operations Regulations 1992). Some of the statutory justifications for the use of risk assessments originate from this legislation. Various other legislation, including the Employment Rights Act 1996 and the Control of Major Accident Hazards (COMAH) Regulations 1999, requires employers and/or employees to take care to prevent dangerous circumstances, and again this may impact on the use of restrictive physical interventions.

Two perspectives within the employment legislation apply to the use of restrictive physical interventions. On the one hand there is a requirement to prevent dangerous occurrences in workplaces (which may be used to justify their use). On the other hand there are requirements to keep employees safe (which imply that if staff use them they must be able to apply them properly and safely – this again suggesting that there is a need for good quality training).

Mental Capacity Act 2005 This Act, which came into force in April 2007, provides a statutory framework to empower and protect adults who lack capacity to make some decisions for themselves. It embodies the principles of 'best interests' and 'least restrictive option'. Section 5 of the Act offers statutory protection from liability where a person is performing an act in connection with the care or treatment of someone who lacks capacity. Section 6 of the Act sets out limitations on Section 5, defines 'restraint' and says that it is only permitted if the person using it reasonably believes it is necessary to prevent harm to the person who lacks capacity, and if the restraint used is a proportionate response to the likelihood and the seriousness of the harm. This section of the Act does not cover the deprivation of liberty.

The Mental Health Act 2007 amended the Mental Capacity Act 2005 and the Mental Health Act 1983 to provide additional safeguards for people who are deprived of their liberty without a formal legal sanction (ie on a 'voluntary basis') but who lack capacity to make their own decisions about where and how they will be cared for. The Act sets out to implement the so-called 'Bournewood Safeguards' and covers any adult suffering from a mental disorder who is unable to give informed consent to their care (ie lacking capacity) and for whom deprivation of liberty is considered, after an independent assessment, to be necessary and in their best interests to protect them from harm. The Department of Health and Ministry of Justice have consulted on a proposed code of practice to support the safeguards applicable to England and Wales and on regulations applicable to England.

Capacity is a complex issue. The Mental Health Act Code of Practice (DoH/Welsh Office, 1993) says, in relation to consent to medical treatment, that for an individual to have capacity they must be able to:

- understand what medical treatment is and that somebody has said that they need it and why treatment is being proposed

- understand in broad terms the nature of the proposed treatment

- understand its principal benefits and risks

- understand what will be the consequences of not receiving the proposed treatment

- possess the capacity to make the choice

These five elements can also be used to test whether or not a person has the capacity to make other decisions, for example to have a sexual relationship or to live with other people. The proposed new law will apply to both public and private placements and will place a duty on the hospital or care home to apply to the supervisory body (the local council) for authorisation to deprive a person (who does not have capacity) of their liberty. There will also be a review process. This legislation may be relevant to the use of restrictive physical interventions though much will depend on the definition of 'deprivation of liberty' that is used. It is envisaged that locking of doors would not, in itself, be sufficient to meet this definition.

Some relevant guidance and circulars

Guidance on the Use of Permissible Forms of Control in Children's Residential Care and Regulation 8 (2) of the Children's Homes Regulations 1991

This guidance, issued in 1992, refers to all children, and not specifically to those with learning disabilities, who have severe challenging behaviour and only applies to public and independent sector children's homes. The guidance defines 'physical restraint' as 'the positive application of force with the intention of overpowering the child in order to protect the child from harming himself or others or seriously damaging property'. It states which sanctions can be used and the procedures that should be followed when using them. The guidance points out that the only provisions of the Children Act 1989 that permit the restriction of the liberty of a child or young person are the ones relating to the use of secure accommodation. Lesser forms of restriction of liberty or restraint should only be used where immediate action is necessary to prevent injury to a person or damage to property, and they should not be used as a punishment or purely to enforce compliance with the instructions of members of staff. Paragraph 8.3 of the guidance acknowledges that where children have an impaired ability to recognise and understand danger there may be a need for more frequent use of restraint or physical interventions.

Section 93 of the Education and Inspections Act 2006 replaces Section 550A of the Education Act 1996 and gives powers to members of staff in schools to use reasonable force to prevent any pupil from:

- committing an offence

- causing personal injury to, or damage to the property of, any person (including the pupil himself)

- prejudicing the maintenance of good order and discipline in the school or among any pupils receiving education at the school, whether during a teaching session or otherwise

This section applies to any person who is, in relation to a pupil, a member of staff of any school at which education is provided for the pupil. It applies on the school premises and elsewhere if the member of staff has lawful control or charge of the pupil concerned. The legislation does not sanction the use of corporal punishment. New guidance was published by the Department for Children, Schools and Families (which replaced DfES) in November 2007 to support this new legislation. It is important for staff working in school settings to become fully conversant with this guidance.

DfES Circular 10/98 provides detailed guidance on the interpretation of the Education Act 1996. It provides examples of situations that fall within the three categories of incident (described above) that may justify the use of reasonable force. Though recognising that ultimately this could be a matter for the courts to decide, it offers guidance on what is meant by 'reasonable force'. It gives advice on the use of force and on the kinds of actions that may be appropriate. It provides detailed advice on the recording of incidents. Finally, it provides advice about the circumstances in which physical contact with pupils may or may not be appropriate.

National Minimum Standards (NMS) These standards for care services published by the Department of Health under Section 23(1) of the Care Standards Act 2000 are not, in themselves, legally binding but they provide important benchmarks in defining what activities are 'reasonable'. NMS 23.5 of the standards for care homes for younger adults says that in order to ensure that service users are protected from abuse, neglect and self-harm care providers must ensure that '*physical and verbal aggression by a service user is understood and dealt with appropriately, and physical intervention is only used as a last resort by trained staff in accordance with Department of Health guidance, protects the rights and best interests of the service user, and is the minimum consistent with safety*'. The NMS for domiciliary care agencies, care homes for older people and children's homes all contain almost identical provisions. The NMS for children's homes also go into greater detail, for example requiring the production of policies and effective recording of incidents.

Guidance on Restrictive Physical Interventions for People with Learning Disability and Autistic Spectrum Disorder in Health, Education and Social Care Settings 2002 This guidance, issued jointly by the Department of Health and the Department for Education and Skills, is one of the most recent and relevant documents applicable to the use of restrictive physical interventions in care settings. As such, readers are strongly encouraged to obtain and carefully read a copy of it. It can be found on the Department of Health website. The document emphasises that provider agencies need effective policies, procedures and training for staff who work with people who may have behavioural episodes where restrictive physical intervention is necessary to ensure their safety and that of others. It promotes the concept of including potential strategies and actions in care plans, to help staff and people who use services deal effectively with such episodes. It emphasises the use of training organisations with relevant expertise and experience. It also emphasises the importance of the use of risk assessments in order to justify using restrictive physical interventions.

Statutory arrangements for the safeguarding of vulnerable adults also provide an important context within which the use of restrictive physical interventions must be considered since inappropriate use is likely to be viewed as abuse within the terms of this framework. Three key components are:

- the arrangements for the multi-agency investigation of alleged incidents of abuse that are set out in Local Authority Circular LAC(2000)7 *No Secrets* and good practice guidance published by the Association of Directors of Social Services *Safeguarding Adults: A National Framework of Standards for Good Practice and Outcomes in Adult Protection Work* and the various Department of Education and Skills publications on safeguarding children

- the arrangements for the criminal record vetting of all people working with vulnerable adults and children

- the system for maintaining national lists of people judged to be unsuitable to work with vulnerable adults and children

The issues arising from the Bichard Inquiry (June 2004) were addressed through the Safeguarding Vulnerable Groups Act 2006 that laid the foundation for a new Independent Safeguarding Authority scheme.

The Welsh Assembly Government published the guidance note *Framework for Restrictive Physical Intervention Policy and Practice* in March 2005. There are many similarities between the requirements for the use of restraint in regulated care services in Wales and those in England. For example, The Care Homes (Wales) Regulations 2002 say:

- *The registered person shall ensure that no service user is subject to physical restraint unless restraint of the kind employed is the only practicable means of securing the welfare of that or any other service user and there are exceptional circumstances. (Clause 7)*

- *On any occasion on which a service user is subject to physical restraint, the registered person shall record the circumstances, including the nature of the restraint. (Clause 8)*

Readers in Wales are encouraged to consult the website of the Care and Social Services Inspectorate Wales.

Can restrictive physical interventions be classed as treatment?

As well as being used to avoid or minimise the adverse consequences of violent or reckless behaviour, restrictive physical interventions may be employed as part of a broader treatment strategy to overcome severe challenging behaviours. For example, if a person typically responds to instruction by engaging in severe self-injury it may be considered appropriate to use a restrictive physical intervention during teaching sessions. In these circumstances, the restrictive physical intervention would not only be a means of preventing harm but would also be part of a strategy to overcome the person's failure to co-operate in an educational or treatment programme. The alternative would be not to teach the person new behaviours and, by implication, to accept all the limitations to personal growth and development imposed by the presence of challenging behaviours.

In these circumstances, it can be argued that a failure to employ an appropriate treatment by withholding a relevant restrictive physical intervention might be construed as a breach of a legal duty of care. However, there is, as yet, no legal or professional consensus as to whether or not a restrictive physical intervention can be considered as part of a treatment programme. Until this is more clearly established, it seems unlikely that any service will be required to provide a legal defence for *not* introducing a restrictive physical intervention. In contrast, a duty of care lays a responsibility upon provider agencies to take reasonable measures to protect staff and/or service users from injury and to prevent damage to property.

The law in Scotland

Criminal law

Although there are many similarities between the English and Scottish legal systems, there are also substantial differences. Scottish courts are not bound by precedent in the same way that English courts are.

Assault Unlike in the English legislation where physical contact must occur for an offence of assault to have taken place, the Scottish definition of an 'assault' requires that physical contact between the offender and the victim is likely or possible. However, the victim does not have to be injured as a result of the attack or physical threats. Because an assault is defined in Scotland as a crime of intent, it cannot be committed accidentally or recklessly or negligently. It is possible that the use of a restrictive physical intervention that starts out as a lawful act could become an assault if the state of mind of the person using the intervention changes from seeking to control a service user's behaviour, to intentionally inflicting pain or punishment. This is the concept of '*mens rea*', the mental element of the execution of a criminal act.

Culpable and reckless conduct The unintentional causing of harm or injury to an individual as a result of accident or negligence is not necessarily a crime in Scotland unless it is accompanied by recklessness. Where recklessness can be demonstrated possible offences include: cruel and barbarous treatment; cruel and unnatural treatment; and causing real injury and reckless injury. There is also the crime of 'recklessly endangering the lieges' that may take place when an individual creates a situation that puts the public in serious danger. This might be relevant when a person with severe challenging behaviour is taken into a public place without adequate planning and safeguards.

Homicide In Scotland 'murder' includes 'any wilful act causing the destruction of life by which the perpetrator either wickedly intends to kill or displays wicked recklessness as to whether the victim lives or dies'. The term 'wicked' is used to mean a proven or admitted intention to kill. The term 'wicked recklessness' refers to the intention of the perpetrator to impose on the victim great bodily harm that might result in death and that shows strong disregard as to whether the victim lives or dies.

'Culpable homicide' is the Scottish version of manslaughter and 'involuntary culpable homicide' can occur where there was no actual intention of taking someone's life (eg as a result of an assault).

Criminal law defences

Reflex action Occasionally the argument that a particular reaction to a situation occurred as a result of a reflex action may be taken into account by a court. This is different from **self-defence** which implies that the perpetrator must perceive that there is an imminent and unavoidable danger to life though the response must not involve excessive violence.

Provocation is a plea that may be possible when self-defence is rejected. It requires some form of violence sustaining injury or harm, a total loss of self-control, the use of force that is proportionate to the provocative act and immediate retaliation to the provocation. Provocation may minimise the severity of a sentence but would not lead to total acquittal.

Diminished responsibility is a possible partial defence for charges of murder and is based on the argument that at the time of the offence the accused was suffering from an abnormality of mind that substantially impaired their ability to determine or control their actions.

Necessity is based on the notion that circumstances may require the accused to commit an illegal or criminal act in order to avoid more severe outcomes that would follow from failing to take any action.

Coercion occurs when a person is forced by another to commit a criminal act. To use this as a defence it would be necessary to demonstrate that the accused believed that he was in immediate danger of death or great bodily harm and so unable to resist. The accused must also play a subordinate part in the crime and not the active role.

Lawful force Scottish law permits parents and others with parental responsibility for a child to exercise lawful force in the exercise of discipline or chastisement though there is a lack of clarity about what constitutes 'reasonable' chastisement. Section 51 of the Criminal Justice (Scotland) Act 2003 plays an important part in identifying what can be regarded as a 'justifiable assault' on a child. It should also be noted that Section 16 of the Standards in Scotland's Schools Act 2000 prohibits the use of any physical chastisement in private and state schools.

Restrain a lunatic In Scotland there is a specific legal acknowledgement of the common law power of individuals to 'restrain a lunatic' for a short period where there is evidence of danger or risk of personal injury.

Civil law

Delict In Scotland, a wrongful action committed by one person against another is known as a 'delict' and may render the wrongdoer liable to pay compensation (reparation) to the victim. The legislative basis is the Law of Obligations which encompasses the rights and obligations that underpin relationships between private individuals. These obligations can be voluntary, resulting from agreements (including contracts) between parties, or involuntary or 'obediential where the obligation is created by the law. The latter apply to relationships between carers and people who use services.

Assault is an intentional delict that, unlike in criminal cases, does not have to include 'evil' intent and does not necessarily imply physical contact or damage. In civil law, consent given by an individual who has capacity to give such consent negates the delict of assault. Self-defence, unavoidable accident and consent are some of the defences that may be applicable when arguing that an assault has not taken place.

False imprisonment, detention and restraint Scottish civil law also encompasses injuries to liberty such as false imprisonment, detention and restraint. Again, there are defences that may be used to justify such actions. These include lawful arrest and statutory powers to detain people who are mentally ill.

Fear and force The delict of fear and force covers circumstances where an individual is verbally or physically intimidated, threatened or bullied to act in a way that they would not normally do.

Negligence is an unintentional delict that has to have an element of 'fault' that can be unintended as well as deliberate. This is relevant to a carer who acts in a way that would not be judged reasonable by other carers. Duty of care is an important determinant in such cases. Negligence is also measured against the concept of **standard of care** which is defined as 'the actions that a reasonable person would take in a given situation'. When considering negligence claims, Scottish courts will take into account the likelihood and seriousness of harm resulting from an action and the practicality and cost of precautions.

Care professionals may also be sued for delictual liability if the actions they take can be demonstrated to fall below the standard of care expected of a reasonable member of the profession. A key issue here is the extent to which it is possible to arrive at a common view about the appropriate standard of professional care.

Civil law defences

As in criminal law, there are a number of defences that can be used when it is argued that a civil offence has been committed in Scotland:

Volenti not fit injuria covers the idea that the person who has suffered injury has already accepted the risks involved and absolved the perpetrator from the consequences of negligence. This may be relevant to the use of planned restrictive physical interventions that are included in a properly devised care plan.

Contributory negligence may reduce the level of responsibility of a care giver if it can be demonstrated that the victim was negligent too. **Joint fault** is a similar defence that may be used to mitigate the consequence to an individual perpetrator by arguing that other people were equally involved.

Employment Law

Where an employer and an employee can be shown to have a contract of employment (as opposed merely to a contract to provide a service) the employer may have a vicarious liability for any wrongful conduct of an employee during the course of employment that results in the injury of a third party. The Scottish courts have established that such a liability is likely to exist where the employee has authorised the action, and this applies even when the employee carries out the task in a way the employer would not endorse. However, there is less likelihood of the employer being held responsible when the action is clearly outside the scope of the work the person is employed to do or where the employer's resources are used for the employees' own purposes without permission.

The concept of employer's liability applies in Scotland in much the same way as it does in England. Workplace health and safety legislation is a matter that is reserved to the UK Parliament. The power to make or change health and safety legislation has not been devolved to the Scottish Parliament.

Human rights law

The Scotland Act 1998, which established the Scottish Parliament and the Scottish Executive, requires these two bodies to comply with the European Convention on Human Rights and not to enact any legislation that contravenes these rights. The Human Rights Act 1998 applies in Scotland.

Relevant legislation and guidance

Adults with Incapacity (Scotland) Act 2000 This Act provides guidance on the making of decisions about the welfare, property and finances of adults who are legally incapable and its aim is to promote their freedom and autonomy as much as possible. It is underpinned by the notion that although a person may be judged incapable in one situation this does not have to mean that they are incapable in others. The Act aims to ensure that decisions taken to promote the well-being of adults with mental incapacity are not so controlling and all-embracing as to become over-protective and potentially abusive. The Act sets out a number of principles that must be taken into account when making these decisions and these must be reflected in any policies and case decisions about the care of such vulnerable adults. It is important for people involved in the provision of care in Scotland to familiarise themselves with these principles and this legislation.

Mental Health (Care and Treatment) (Scotland) Act 2003 This Act also needs to be taken into account as it indicates that use of force or detention must be immediately necessary and is only permissible for so long as it is necessary in the circumstances. The legislation raises questions about the extent to which people can make advance directives that sanction the use of restrictive physical interventions.

In 1999 the Scottish Executive published guidance prepared by the Scottish Office Education and Industry Department entitled *Helping Hands: Guidelines for Staff who Provide Intimate Care for Children and Young People with Disabilities.* The document covers the use of restraint.

Arising from the inquiry into the death of David Bennett, a psychiatric in-patient in Norfolk, the Scottish Executive reviewed the findings of the report to ascertain whether there were any lessons for Scotland's mental health services and published *Safe Care: Consideration of the Recommendations from the Inquiry (England) into the Death of David Bennett* (Scottish Executive, 2006) containing 22 recommendations for action. Though primarily directed at mental health services, a number of the recommendations have wider applicability including:

- the need for cultural awareness and sensitivity and for training in tackling racism

- a range of recommendations to ensure that services respond appropriately to the diverse needs of black and minority ethnic groups

- arrangements for a national system of training in the use of restrictive physical interventions (though this idea has not yet been implemented)

- arrangements for the proper recording and monitoring of the use of restraint (with a particular focus on those interventions that result in injuries)

- the provision of further training to ensure staff are aware of the risks associated with the overuse of medication

There are many parallels between the regulatory systems in England and Scotland. The Regulation of Care (Scotland) Act 2001 includes provisions for the making of Regulations and National Minimum Standards that cover all regulated care services for adults and children. Regulation 4(c) of the Regulation of Care (Requirements as to Care Services) (Scotland) Regulations 2002 requires care providers to *'ensure that no service user is subject to restraint unless it is the only practicable means of securing the welfare of that or any other service user and there are exceptional circumstances'*. National Minimum Standard 9 of the care homes for people with learning disabilities requires staff to *'record and investigate... any episodes of restraint'* and says that people who use services should be able to be *'confident that staff will not use restraint at all unless it is permitted by law and even then restraint will not be used until other interventions have failed (unless it is legally required)'*. There are similar provisions for other service user groups, for example The Residential Establishments – Child Care (Scotland) Regulations 1996 contain similar provisions for children. Regulation 10 is particularly relevant.

The Scottish Institute for Residential Child Care handbook *Holding Safely: A Guide for Residential Child Care Practitioners and Managers about Physically Restraining Children and Young People* (Davidson et al, 2005) provides guidance for managers and practitioners about physically restraining children and young people. It gives comprehensive coverage of the subject with a very practical focus. Appendix 4 of *Holding Safely* provides information about legal matters. The publication *Safe and Well: Good Practice in Schools and Education Authorities for Keeping Children Safe and Well* (Scottish Executive, 2005) also includes practice advice for schools and educational authorities about the use of restraint. In Scotland the term restraint is still used in preference to restrictive physical interventions.

Replacing guidance published earlier (Mental Welfare Commission for Scotland, 2002), *Rights, Risks and Limits to Freedom* (Mental Welfare Commission for Scotland, 2006) addresses principles and good practice guidance for practitioners considering restraining adults in residential care settings. The approach adopted sets out that:

- restraint should be seen as a 'last resort'

- some degree of risk-taking is an essential part of good care

- restraint must never be used as a threat in order to control behaviour

- staff need to consider the balance between their residents' self-determination and the duty to care

- human interactions are central to the provision of good quality care

- the use of restraint must comply with the law

Appendix 1 of *Rights, Risks and Limits to Freedom* looks at relevant Scottish legislation in some detail. It builds on principles set out in the 2002 document:

- Wherever possible, people who use services should participate in decisions about how and when they should be restrained.

- There should be a full risk assessment, incorporated in the service user's care plan, aimed at understanding why the behaviours occur.

- The degree of acceptable risk must be established.

- Alternatives to applying restrictive physical interventions must always be considered first.

- Where restraint is applied it should always be at the minimum effective level and for the minimum time.

- There must be a process of continuous monitoring and review of the use of restrictive physical interventions.

- Where unplanned intervention is used there should be full support and an explanation should be given to the service user as soon as possible after the event.

- Its use must be carefully monitored (and this is underpinned by a need for thorough and timely recording of incidents).

Conclusions

This chapter has provided a brief overview of some of the legal issues arising from the use of restrictive physical interventions with children and adults with a learning disability or autistic spectrum disorder. It does not, however, provide a basis for properly establishing the legality of specific procedures employed in the management of challenging behaviour. This will depend on the particular circumstances, including the behaviours giving concern, and the range of interventions already employed. Where services have concerns about the legal status of procedures employed to respond to challenging behaviours they are advised to consult a lawyer with relevant experience.

In protecting the rights of individuals the law makes an important contribution to establishing standards of care within services. This can be summarised in the form of two underlying principles:

Key policy principle 1 Any restrictive physical intervention should be consistent with the legal obligations and responsibilities of care agencies and their staff and the rights and protection afforded to people with learning disabilities under the law.

Key policy principle 2 Working within the 'legal framework', services are responsible for the provision of care, including restrictive physical interventions, which are in the person's best interests.

How these principles are applied in practice will be determined by the characteristics of the person concerned, the quality of local services and the availability of staff expertise. For services that employ restrictive physical interventions the central issues are: prevention of challenging behaviours; using restrictive physical interventions to promote the best interests of service users; assessing the risks associated with restrictive physical interventions; ensuring the safety of service users and staff; discharging the responsibilities of managers and employers; and ensuring that staff are properly trained in the use of restrictive physical interventions. If applied properly all this will lead to practice that would be judged 'reasonable' in the event of any challenges to it. The remainder of this book is concerned with the development of good practice in relation to each of these topics.

Agenda for action

1.   Does your service sanction the use of restrictive physical interventions for adults and/or children? If so, can you provide a justification in respect of both the criminal law and the civil law?

2.   Is your use of restrictive physical interventions consistent with good practice as set out in guidance and circulars by government departments and regulatory bodies?

3.   Are procedures in place to ensure that restrictive physical interventions are always used in the best interests of each individual service user?

Chapter 3
A common values base

Our approach to developing policies to support good practice in the use of restrictive physical interventions is based on the assumption that everyone responsible for commissioning and providing services for people with learning disabilities and/or autism shares common values. These include a commitment to operate within the law and to provide services that adhere to accepted clinical and professional standards. Above all, it is assumed that services operate in the best interests of service users. There is also widespread concern that people with a learning disability have, in the past, been marginalised by society and treated as second-class citizens.

The governments of England, Wales and Scotland have all sought to identify shared values that can provide a moral and ethical reference point for service development and innovation. *Valuing People*, the English Government White Paper (2001), referred to rights, independence, inclusion and choice. In Scotland *The Same as You* report identified seven principles that included people with learning disabilities being valued, treated as individuals, being encouraged to contribute to the community they live in, having choices, using the same services as other people and receiving appropriate support. From these two examples it should be clear that while values can be described in relatively abstract terms (*Valuing People*) or in a more practical way (*The Same as You*), the underlying concepts are very similar.

The outline presented here is based on work by Blunden (Blunden, 1988; Blunden and Allen, 1987) and the National Autistic Society.

Rights and entitlements

Every service user has the rights or entitlements set out below.

Physical well-being

- a healthy lifestyle including a nutritious and balanced diet, exercise, medical assistance and dental care

- not to be exposed to unreasonable risk

- reasonable protection from injury

- freedom from ill-treatment and abuse including the misuse of medication

- medical needs and medication regularly reviewed

- appropriate care in relation to hygiene and physical comfort

- freedom from sexual abuse or exploitation

Emotional well-being

- access to the same range of activities and pastimes as non-disabled people of a similar age and background

- be treated fairly and with courtesy and respect

- have new experiences and opportunities for learning that are appropriate to their interests and abilities

- make choices and be involved in making decisions that affect their lives

- have respect from others for their cultural and religious background

Material well-being

- own personal possessions

- possess comfortable clothes that reflect their age, gender, race and personal preferences

- access to mobility aids and transport

- live in a comfortable, clean and safe home

Social well-being

- be accepted by others

- opportunities for meeting other people including those without disabilities

- opportunities to form close (including sexual) relationships

- opportunities for religious observance

- representation where decisions that affect them are made either directly or with support from an advocate who is independent of the service provider

- privacy

- access to confidential advice and support

Quality can best be measured by the way in which services influence the quality of life of service users (Perry and Felce, 1995). Most services, quite rightly, concentrate on positive efforts to maintain or increase the quality of life of service users. However, any decision to use restrictive physical interventions requires a framework that considers the potential for both positive and negative outcomes for service users. In this book it is assumed that service quality will be enhanced by the development of policies that make explicit reference to the well-being or best interest of service users.

Four central values

A person's well-being is likely to be put at risk when restrictive physical interventions are used inappropriately or without due consideration to the person's best interests and it is an adherence to underlying values that ultimately offers protection against poor practice or abuse. There is not sufficient space here to consider how each of the rights and entitlements set out above might be compromised by restrictive physical interventions. Instead, this chapter focuses on four central values that are frequently referred to in service policies. Where restrictive physical interventions are employed, careful consideration should be given to these values. Readers are invited to review the possible impact of restrictive physical interventions on other rights and entitlements of individual service users.

Best interests

This is the general or superordinate principle that links the legal framework with good practice in service settings. In the event of a legal challenge about the use of a restrictive physical intervention, the service agency or organisation would be expected to provide evidence to show how the procedures promoted the service user's best interests. The policy framework described here can be used to promote good practice and ensure that appropriate evidence is available to support the principle of best interest.

Key policy principle

3

Restrictive physical interventions should only be used in the best interests of the service user.

 Good practice

Sam is ten years old and has a profound learning disability and cerebral palsy. He is only able to concentrate on any one activity for short periods and, when not occupied, he frequently interferes with the work of other pupils. The physiotherapist has recommended that Sam is placed in a standing frame for ten minutes at a time when he is undertaking a programme designed to improve his hand–eye co-ordination. While Sam is in the standing frame, his freedom of movement is severely restricted. The standing frame is a restrictive physical intervention to promote Sam's education and development. It is used in his best interest.

 Poor practice

When Sam is in the standing frame, he is unable to move around the classroom and interfere with other pupils. Sam's teacher leaves him in the frame for longer and longer periods of time. The decision to extend the time Sam spends in the frame is based on the teacher's concerns about classroom organisation – not what is best for Sam.

Fair treatment

When people with learning disabilities present challenging behaviours, it may be difficult for staff to maintain warm and positive relationships. Positive attitudes and values may be gradually undermined. Staff may be tempted to use inappropriate forms of restrictive physical intervention that undermine a person's self-respect. The use of restrictive physical interventions can easily become an opportunity for staff to express underlying feelings of resentment or anger that have accumulated over a period of time.

Key policy principle

4

Service users should be treated fairly and with courtesy and respect.

 Good practice

Beth is seventeen but she has no appreciation of the dangers posed by traffic. When she is out with members of staff she often tries to run across busy roads. The staff have discussed their concerns with Beth and have agreed that when they go into town Beth will always walk on the inside of the pavement with a member of staff between her and the road. The member of staff walks close to Beth with her arm looped over Beth's arm. Beth is happy with this arrangement and rarely tries to break away when she is accompanied like this. If she tries to break away, the member of staff will tighten her hold on Beth's arm and place one arm firmly around her waist.

 Poor practice

Mary is twenty-three and has a fascination for puddles. On a wet day she seeks out puddles and stamps in them until she is completely soaked and dirty. To avoid this, staff insist that if Mary goes out in the rain she wears a wrist strap with one end held by a member of staff. If she goes near a puddle she is warned not to be 'dirty' or 'childish'.

Involved decision-making

The decision to use a restrictive physical intervention often involves actions that override a service user's free will. For example, it may be necessary to hold the hands of a person who is self-injuring. The desirability for control in one aspect of a person's life can easily lead on to the assumption that staff should exert control in other areas. For example, it might be assumed that the person need not be consulted about the use of a restrictive physical intervention or that staff should make decisions about other activities unrelated to the use of restrictive physical interventions.

Key policy principle 5   Service users should be helped to make choices and be involved in making decisions that affect their lives.

 Good practice

When Will first began attending the social and education centre he found it very difficult to wait in line for drinks and meals in the cafeteria. Often he would shout and become aggressive to other people who were waiting in line and on two occasions members of staff had to hold his arms and take him to another room to calm down. As soon as they recognised that Will found it frustrating to wait in line, the staff talked to him about ways of overcoming the problem. Will decided to visit the canteen at times when it wasn't busy. He also agreed to try and learn some simple routines to cope with his frustration.

 Poor practice

The first day Jess arrived at his new home he had a temper tantrum in the kitchen because he couldn't find a cup. After that the staff decided that he couldn't be trusted in the kitchen. For the next few months the door was kept locked and he had to ask every time he wanted to use the kitchen.

Appropriate opportunities for learning

Often it is people with very low levels of ability and poor social skills who experience restrictive physical interventions. Sometimes, the use of restrictive physical interventions is seen as evidence that the person is incapable of learning new skills or developing. To avoid this kind of defeatism it is essential that restrictive physical interventions are always combined with a carefully planned programme of educational, social and recreational activities.

Key policy principle

6

There should be experiences and opportunities for learning that are appropriate to the person's interests and abilities.

 Good practice

Andy is frequently aggressive towards himself. Functional analysis has shown that self-injury occurs most often when staff try to involve him in household tasks. Staff are working with a clinical psychologist to identify which activities Andy is able to tolerate without self-injury and to teach him a sign to request more help with tasks he finds difficult.

 Poor practice

Jenny spends a lot of time rocking in a corner. She wears a helmet to discourage her from banging her head on hard objects. If she is approached by staff she usually stops rocking and begins to bang her head on the floor or wall. Staff have agreed that Jenny really wants to be left alone.

Occasionally, challenging behaviours prevent the service user being exposed to new experiences or structured learning opportunities and it may be argued that a restrictive physical intervention, such as holding a person's hands to prevent them striking themselves, or sitting them in a chair close to a desk or table so that they cannot stand up and walk away, are reasonable short-term strategies to achieve longer term goals. It may be argued that such a proactive use of a restrictive physical intervention is in the person's best interest because there is only a limited restriction on his or her freedom of movement for a relatively short period of time. Without the imposition of these restrictions there would be very little prospect of behavioural change or bringing about an overall improvement in the person's quality of life. If such restrictions are accepted as a necessary condition for learning, then other long-term benefits are likely to follow.

Such an approach is problematic because it brings two basic values into direct conflict: a restrictive physical intervention is used to ensure that the person participates in learning, or is at least exposed to new experiences, when their behaviour indicates that they would prefer not to have this experience. There is no simple or clear-cut response to this dilemma. However, any such decision made on behalf of a person who presents challenging behaviour will need to consider the following:

- What steps have been taken to involve the person in making a decision about whether or not to participate?

- What evidence is there to indicate whether or not the person has the capacity to make such a decision?

- For how long will the restrictive physical intervention be used during any one session, or learning experience; how many sessions are planned; and over what period of time?

- What precisely are the long-term benefits for the person likely to be?

- What information will be collected to show whether or not the approach is working?

- How will the decision to use restrictive physical interventions in this way be made and by whom?

Agenda for action

1. Are you clear about how the restrictive physical intervention helps the person concerned, ie is it used in their best interests?

2. Are there any conflicts of interest where you or members of staff experience fewer demands or less stress when the restrictive physical intervention is used?

3. Are the service users who experience restrictive physical interventions consulted before they are used?

4. What steps have been taken to ensure that the restrictive physical interventions minimise any loss of dignity for those concerned?

5. How far and in what ways do the restrictive physical interventions you employ reduce the person's opportunities for choice and making decisions?

6. What steps have been taken to reduce the likelihood that restrictive physical interventions will be needed in future?

7. What has been done to ensure that the use of restrictive physical interventions is combined with opportunities for new experiences and opportunities for learning?

Chapter 4
Prevention of violence and aggression

Restrictive physical interventions should only be used after other, less intrusive, methods have been fully explored and are not adequate to meet the current needs of the service user. An important first step is to examine how behaviours that might be seen as justifying the use of restrictive physical interventions can be prevented. By preventing behaviours that are regarded as dangerous to the service user or to other people, it is possible to minimise the extent to which restrictive physical interventions are employed.

Restrictive physical interventions should not be seen as discrete self-contained procedures that are introduced as a package when behaviour escalates to unacceptable levels. Rather, they should be introduced as part of a graduated response within a holistic programme that seeks to minimise conflict and avoid confrontation between service user and staff. (This is described in more detail in Chapter 7.) It is important to demonstrate that restrictive physical interventions are only used when other less intrusive approaches have been fully explored. Similarly, the more extreme forms of restrictive physical intervention should only be adopted when other less restrictive measures have been tried and found to be inadequate.

Consider the following episode:

Jim shares a house with four other people with learning disabilities. One morning recently he woke up with a heavy cold, feeling tired and irritable. Even on a good day he doesn't like to be hurried, but there were staff shortages and everyone seemed to be rushing around. The staff who usually work with Jim know that if he is asked to do something he responds best to simple verbal instructions and lots of gestures. On this particular morning a new relief worker asked Jim to get some clean towels from the airing cupboard: 'Jim, pop upstairs and get me three clean towels, not hand towels; they're on the middle shelf. Oh, and bring down a clean shirt for yourself while you're there'. Jim knew that he was expected to do something, but he wasn't sure what. As he stood looking confused, the member of staff said, 'Come on Jim, we're running late you know'. Jim began to feel uneasy and under pressure. The member of staff came up close to him and said, 'Jim we need some clean towels, NOW!' Jim resolved a confusing situation where he felt under pressure in the only way he knows. He lashed out and punched the member of staff in the face.

The incident report begins 'For no apparent reason...'

It is clear from the short summary provided that there were factors that combined to push Jim into a violent response. These include:

- personal factors relating to his cold and feelings of irritability
- Jim's difficulty in understanding complicated language
- the sense of hurry and confusion
- Jim's anxiety level, which increased following the staff pressure on him

These factors are referred to as 'setting conditions'.

Key policy principle 7 Challenging behaviours can often be prevented by careful management of the setting conditions.

Setting conditions

It is helpful to consider two types of setting conditions: environmental setting conditions and personal setting conditions. It is then possible to consider how the two types of setting condition interact to produce challenging behaviours.

Environmental setting conditions

In general, the more positive opportunities that are presented for meeting the needs of service users, the less likely it is that aggressive, violent and disruptive behaviours will occur. When there is a mismatch between a person's needs and the opportunities and supports available to them, they are likely to become bored, frustrated, angry or simply confused. If they do not have other ways of expressing themselves, people with learning disabilities and/or autism are likely to react by becoming excitable, overactive and aggressive. For others, violent behaviour is a reaction to distress and panic. Over time, violence or aggression may become the most effective means of influencing the behaviour of other people.

Just as needs vary from person to person, so too will the opportunities and supports that ensure those needs are met. However, there are factors that are likely to influence most service users. Unless these factors are addressed, there is an increased likelihood of violence and aggression occurring. Consider the questions set out in the checklist below:

✔ Checklist

Environmental setting conditions

1   Do staff and carers interact with service users in ways that take account of their strengths and needs?

2   Do service users have access to sufficient space – especially if they like to move around a great deal or to spend time on their own away from other people?

3   Do service users have their own room where personal possessions can be safely kept?

4   Are there opportunities for activities that reflect service users' interests and abilities?

5   Do all service users have individual programme plans that are regularly monitored?

6   Do service users understand what activities are scheduled for each day? What happens if there is an unforeseen change of plan? How are the alternative arrangements explained?

7   Is the environment clean?

8   Is the environment too quiet or too noisy?

9   Are service users provided with full physical check-ups, including eye tests and hearing tests, on a regular basis?

10   Have service users who are receiving medication had their drugs reviewed in the last three months?

11   Are the staff positive, calm, flexible and enjoying their work?

This is not a complete list of the potential setting conditions for violent or disruptive behaviour. However, it illustrates the range of factors that need to be considered. If any of these questions meet with negative responses or the answer is unclear, further work is needed on prevention before restrictive physical interventions are employed.

Personal setting conditions

Our basic biological and psychological make-up is what makes each person different. These differences influence how each one of us reacts to changes in our environment, for example how we respond to the disappointment of a cancelled party or to the frustration of waiting in a queue at the supermarket. There are numerous personal factors that make service users more or less likely to engage in challenging behaviours. In the episode involving Jim, communication difficulties were compounded by the effects of a heavy cold.

Consider the questions about personal setting conditions set out in the checklist below.

✔ Checklist

Personal setting conditions

1   Does the person have difficulty in using spoken language or understanding what other people say? If the person uses signs, are they able to communicate effectively with staff and friends?

2   Does the person have any difficulties with sight or hearing?

3   Does the person suffer from medical conditions such as premenstrual tension, allergies or epilepsy?

4   Does the person have a history of mental illness or anxiety?

5   Is the person receiving any medication such as antipsychotic drugs (eg chlorpromazine, haloperidol) or sedatives (eg diazepam)?

6   Has the person experienced any major life changes during the last year (eg change of residence, bereavement, hospitalisation)?

7   Is it known that the person finds it difficult to cope with certain kinds of experience (eg change in routine, crowds, lots of noise, heights)?

Once again, this list is not exhaustive, but it provides an indication of the areas that need to be considered before restrictive physical interventions are introduced.

Interaction between setting conditions

Of course, personal and environmental setting conditions do not usually occur in isolation. In most cases challenging behaviour occurs because of a particular combination of personal and environmental factors. Often, it is necessary to understand the personal setting conditions for a service user before it is possible to address the relevant environmental conditions. Consider how the setting conditions for Jim were quite specific to his inability to follow complex instructions and his irritability.

Many episodes of challenging behaviour are triggered by a specific event. This may be something very ordinary which acquires special significance because of the setting events. For Jim it was the member of staff demanding a response to a request that he didn't understand. On any other morning Jim might have ignored the demand. If Jim was with his usual staff supporter he probably wouldn't have had these demands placed upon him. But with a new member of staff and a heavy cold, etc it was the last straw.

The interaction between personal and environmental setting conditions and 'triggers' is illustrated in Figure 2.

Figure 2

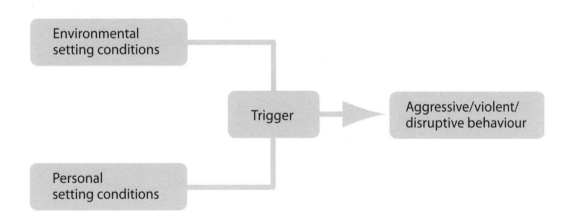

Key policy principle 8 The interaction between environmental setting conditions and personal setting conditions should be explored for each service user who presents a challenge and setting conditions should be modified to reduce the likelihood of challenging behaviours occurring.

Prevention

Primary prevention

Primary prevention involves changing aspects of the person's living and working environment to reduce the likelihood that challenging behaviour will occur. Stages in the development of a primary prevention strategy are shown in the following checklist.

✔ **Checklist**

Primary prevention

1   Analyse environmental and personal setting conditions for each service user.

2   Take steps to ensure that service users are not exposed to situations where personal and environmental setting conditions occur together.

3   Identify triggers for aggression and violence.

4   Avoid the presentation of triggers at critical periods.

5   Change the environment to minimise the likelihood of serious harm.

6   Help the person develop behaviours that lead to positive experiences.

7   Consider whether the person's behaviour could be influenced by personal conditions such as hunger, thirst, pain (earache, headache, toothache), the need to go to the toilet, or environmental setting conditions such as excessive heat, cold or noise.

Good practice

Fawzia becomes extremely anxious unless she knows what is going to happen next ('uncertainty' is a personal factor for Fawzia). If she is left waiting or if arrangements are changed suddenly, she sometimes reacts violently (periods of waiting and changed arrangements are environmental factors). Staff have made a pictorial timetable to show Fawzia the sequence of events during each day.

Ben has poor vision and hearing (personal factors). If he is suddenly interrupted while watching television he becomes very distressed and often hits out (sudden interruptions while Ben is watching television are probably 'triggers' for hitting out). Staff have been briefed to avoid these triggers by approaching Ben gradually and giving him plenty of warning.

Jasmin will sometimes 'bash' her head on the corners of furniture. Staff have changed the environment to minimise serious harm by arranging for the furniture to be changed so that there are no sharp edges that could cause Jasmin serious injury.

Doug has few social skills and generally resists any attempt to participate in group activities. Instead, he sits in a corner rocking and humming to himself. One member of staff has been given time to get to know Doug and to help him learn some basic social interaction skills which could lead to him having more positive experiences.

Walter has very little spoken language. Staff have worked hard to try and understand the non-verbal signals that indicate how Walter feels. Walter has learned a few Makaton signs and symbols to signal 'Stop – that's enough' and 'More – do it again' and the staff try to respond appropriately when he uses these signs. The signs help Walter to change external factors according to how he feels.

Secondary prevention

Secondary prevention concerns the actions taken once a combination of setting conditions and a trigger has precipitated a sequence of behaviours that could escalate into violence or aggression. The aim of secondary prevention is to stop the behaviour building up into a full-blown 'incident'.

Key policy principle

9

Secondary prevention procedures should be established to ensure that problematic episodes are supported appropriately with non-physical interventions before service users become violent or aggressive.

Specific secondary prevention procedures will vary from person to person. Considerations relevant to the development of a strategy for secondary prevention are presented in the following checklist.

 Checklist

Secondary prevention

1　Make options available so that the person isn't boxed into a corner. For example, a person who is upset because they can't watch the television might be interested in a trip to the pub instead. Music, massage or aromatherapy can be soothing for someone who has become agitated and upset.

2　Use physical proximity. For example, will the person be reassured by contact or would they be more relaxed if left alone?

3　Reduce the level of demands. For example, many people become agitated and upset if they are asked to do difficult tasks when they are tired or under the weather. For many people, switching from a high demand task to a low demand leisure activity is a good form of secondary prevention.

4　Change the people who are with the person. For example, challenging behaviour may be associated with lots of people or with very few people in close proximity to the service user. Some service users are more likely to present a challenge when particular people – staff or other service users – are close by.

continued

5   Talk to the person about what concerns them and how they can overcome their difficulty.   For example, it may be that the person is tired of one activity and would like to take a break. Alternatively, they may be helped by encouragement and reassurance that they have almost finished what they set out to do.

6   Be flexible and remember this is not a power struggle.

 ## Good practice

Alex has cerebral palsy, which makes him unsteady and rather clumsy. He is known to have a 'short fuse' and some of the other service users tease him about his poor motor skills. Alex responds by swearing, shouting and eventually kicking. If staff find that the other service users are 'winding Alex up' they immediately suggest an activity that gets Alex away from the rest of the group. They spend a few minutes with Alex reassuring him and reminding him of all the things he is really good at.

When Clive gets tired he becomes increasingly irritable. He often refuses to co-operate and begins to shout and swear at staff. If he is told to 'be quiet' or 'behave properly' he gets gradually more and more upset, pushing people around him and grabbing at their hair or glasses. Staff know that when Clive is like this they should not confront him. Instead, they keep at least ten feet away from him and wait until he calms down. Clive is then given a choice of 'low key' activities, including watching television, to choose from.

Planned and emergency responses to violence and reckless behaviour

Prevention involves foreseeing the possibility of challenging behaviours and taking action to reduce the likelihood that they will actually occur. To this extent prevention is an outcome of risk assessment for each individual service user. A strategy for assessing risk is set out in Chapter 6. Notwithstanding the introduction of preventative measures, there will always be some circumstances that result in violent to aggressive behaviour. However, the information required to implement preventative strategies will also make it more likely that incidents that do occur are anticipated; staff will be able to judge where and when incidents are likely to occur, who is likely to be involved and what kind of challenging behaviour will be displayed. Given this information, it is possible to establish planned procedures that staff should adopt when responding to individual service users who are violent or reckless. Included in the planned procedures should be clear guidance on the use of restrictive physical interventions that may be employed with a particular person.

The development of a comprehensive strategy for responding to challenging behaviours is designed to reduce the use of emergency or unplanned intervention to a minimum. Such a comprehensive strategy will involve:

- primary prevention

- secondary prevention

- planned responses to incidents that do occur

In the absence of a planned response to challenging behaviours, staff have little alternative but to adopt ad hoc emergency strategies. In these circumstances, staff responses should reflect the principles set out for the development of planned restrictive physical interventions. Above all, any use of restrictive physical intervention should involve the minimum amount of force applied for the shortest possible period of time. Staff responses should be guided by judgments about the best interests of the service user. Emergency strategies should immediately set in train a more detailed consideration of the person's challenging behaviour and the development of planned responses in the event of similar behaviours occurring again in the future.

Key policy principle

10

For each service user who presents a challenge there should be individualised strategies for responding to incidents of violence and aggression that, where appropriate, should include directions for using restrictive physical interventions.

It is important that strategies for responding to challenging behaviours are individualised in respect of the person who presents the behaviour and the characteristics of the behaviours themselves. For people who present challenging behaviours in different settings, or in response to different setting conditions, it may be necessary to establish a number of different response strategies.

 Good practice

Zahida and Mandy both display violent behaviour. Staff have established that Zahida gradually becomes violent if she is not allowed to leave an activity when she becomes bored or frustrated. In contrast, Mandy usually starts to hit out at people if her routine is changed unexpectedly. Different strategies have been put in place for preventing the occurrence of challenging behaviours by Zahida and Mandy. Zahida is provided with a choice of alternative activities as soon as she starts to show signs of boredom or frustration and staff are encouraged to talk to her about the things she would like to do. When working with Mandy, staff are expected to anticipate changes in routine so that Mandy can be prepared and provided with other similar activities. Staff have been given clear guidance and training on restrictive physical interventions that may be used with Mandy if she does hit out. Restrictive physical interventions are not needed to manage Zahida's challenging behaviour.

Poor practice

Geoff presents a number of challenging behaviours. If staff make too many demands on him he often hits out. On the other hand, if he is bored he will sometimes rock backwards and forwards so that his head hits a hard surface. Staff have been told that Geoff presents a number of violent behaviours and that, whenever this happens, they should physically remove Geoff to his bedroom to 'cool off'.

Agenda for action

1. Which service users are likely to present violent or reckless behaviour?

2. For each service user:

    ● What are the environmental setting conditions?

    ● What are the personal setting conditions?

    ● What are the triggers for violence and aggression?

3. What primary prevention measures have been taken for each service user?

4. What secondary prevention measures have been taken for each service user?

5. Are there planned strategies for responding to the severe challenging behaviours that do occur?

Chapter 5

Promoting the best interests of service users

Recognising conflicts of interest

A fundamental principle underlying the use of restrictive physical interventions is that they promote the best interests of service users. However, the circumstances that lead up to the use of restrictive physical interventions are likely to involve complex and often emotionally loaded interactions between staff and service users. Under these conditions, it may not always be easy to distinguish between the best interests of the person concerned, the needs of other service users and the personal goals of members of staff. For example, after an episode of escalating aggression leading to physical violence, the use of a restrictive physical intervention will probably result in a reduction in the demands made on staff and a more peaceful environment for other service users. This creates the possibility of conflicting interests for those responsible for decision-making. Staff may be tempted to use restrictive physical interventions primarily to meet their own needs or those of other service users rather than to promote the best interests of the person who presents a challenge (Harris, 1996). It may also be that some service users invoke fear or apprehension in staff, thereby increasing the risk of the use of restrictive physical interventions.

Where restrictive physical interventions are approved for individual service users, it is essential that guidance is available to help staff identify and resolve such conflicts. Policy documents can protect the interests of service users.

Individualised procedures

Working with service users who are violent or unpredictable can be stressful and traumatic for care staff, and the adrenaline levels of both staff and clients are likely to be high. Staff will need to make rapid decisions and work effectively as a team. Well rehearsed procedures for responding to behaviours presented by individual service users will reduce staff anxiety and minimise the risk of injury to staff and other service users. The procedures should enable care staff to respond effectively to violent or aggressive behaviours while ensuring the safety of all concerned. This approach will also ensure that restrictive physical interventions are not used inappropriately or with service users for whom other, less intrusive, methods are effective.

Key policy principle

11

Individualised procedures should be established to enable care staff to respond effectively to service users who are likely to present violent or reckless behaviour while ensuring the safety of all concerned.

 Good practice

Occasionally, Sally becomes extremely violent and destroys furniture and decorations in the house where she lives. At such times both Sally and her carers are at risk of injury. The local multidisciplinary learning disability team has worked with Sally's carers to produce a response plan that sets out exactly how staff should react during these episodes. The plan includes a detailed description of the behaviours that may require restrictive physical interventions, how and when restrictive physical interventions should be introduced, the holds that should be selected, and recording and debriefing procedures. The plan indicates how staff should work together as a team and the ongoing training that all staff involved with Sally should receive. When Sally is calm, staff explain to Sally that the actions taken were to prevent her and others from harm. To do this they use symbols compatible with Sally's level of comprehension.

Poor practice

John has a life-long history of aggression towards other people. The manager at John's house believes that dealing with aggression is 'all part of the job' for the care staff, although she herself rarely works directly with John. Staff have had no guidance on how to respond to violent behaviour and have devised their own methods of restraining John. Consequently, there is no agreement on how violent John is allowed to become before he receives a restrictive physical intervention and different staff use different 'holds'. New staff are expected to learn 'on the job' and often invent their own ways of dealing with John. Both John and staff have received minor injuries during incidents involving aggressive behaviour and the frequency of such incidents is steadily increasing.

Developing a holistic strategy

While restrictive physical interventions may reduce the impact of challenging behaviours, they will never help a person with a learning disability to acquire other more appropriate behaviours. Used in isolation, restrictive physical interventions can easily become self-maintaining. They are an effective response once the behaviour has occurred but, because they do nothing to promote other forms of behaviour, they increase the chances that the challenging behaviour itself is repeated. On rare occasions a service user may actively seek out or encourage the use of restrictive physical interventions. This suggests that the restrictive physical intervention is addressing otherwise unmet needs. When this happens it is important to assess the sensory profile of the service user and consider other ways of providing physical support or contact.

Restrictive physical interventions should always be combined with other strategies that are designed to help the service user learn more appropriate behaviours and ways of communicating their needs. Depending on the service user concerned, a variety of approaches may be employed. Visual symbols or choice cards have been found to be helpful, irrespective of whether or not the person uses spoken language.

Key policy principle 12   Restrictive physical interventions should only be used in conjunction with other strategies designed to help service users learn alternative non-challenging behaviours.

Good practice

Ron has autism and moderate learning disabilities. He has been losing weight and needs a medical examination, during which blood will have to be collected. Ron is terrified of needles and doctors and in the past has refused to co-operate with any form of medical treatment. Staff devise a visual schedule for Ron, showing him what will happen. They then begin a number of visits to the surgery, starting with short visits and slowly building up the time he spends there. The visit is always followed by a visit to Ron's favourite video store. As this routine develops and becomes familiar, Ron begins to relax and his schedule is amended to show people touching him, anaesthetising his arm and eventually introducing the needles. This behaviour is modeled by the accompanying staff. It is always followed by Ron's favourite activity and he soon adjusts to this as part of the routine. After three weeks the doctor is able to obtain the blood sample without causing Ron any distress.

 Poor practice

Joe has severe learning disabilities and requires dental treatment. Staff persuade him to enter the dentist's surgery reassuring him that it won't hurt. Once he is sitting in the dentist's chair, he is held firmly in the chair by three staff while the dentist examines him, administers a local anesthetic and extracts a tooth.

The application of general procedures to adults and children with very different needs will inevitably fail to take account of individual differences. This makes it much less likely that the most appropriate and least intrusive physical interventions will be employed. For example, some people with autism have heightened sensitivity to certain kinds of stimulation. These sensitivities should inform any decision about the use of restrictive physical interventions and the particular 'holds' or techniques employed. Similarly, if a service user actively seeks restrictive physical interventions, care will need to be taken to avoid the intervention becoming a reinforcing consequence of challenging behaviour (Harris, 1996). Before deciding to use any restrictive physical intervention, all potential risks and benefits for the recipient should be identified and other courses of action considered. Restrictive physical interventions should be consistent with professional advice and established good practice.

Good practice

 A person who has uncontrollable outbursts in crowded settings is taught how to relax when under stress.

 Domestic chores are broken down into small steps for a person who uses aggression to escape from difficult tasks.

 A person engaging in self-injurious behaviours has their sensory needs assessed.

 Counselling is provided for a person who has become increasingly violent after the death of a close relative.

 Service users are taught to make choices using media appropriate to their receptive and expressive skills (eg visual communication symbols or photographs).

 A person who lapses into long periods of repetitive self-injury when left alone is provided with a range of activities and involvement with other people.

 A child who often becomes violent when interacting with groups of other children is taught a range of simple social skills.

 A teenage girl who found it very difficult to be close to adult men without becoming aggressive was taught some simple relaxation routines.

 Poor practice

Ruth has not been involved in any structured educational activities for the past two years because staff feel this precipitates aggressive outbursts. When she does become aggressive Ruth is restrained in a 'Buxton chair'.

Anwar has been prone to violent temper tantrums all his life and staff routinely apply arm holds and wrist locks to prevent him hitting out. It is well known that he is usually aggressive when frustrated by his inability to communicate simple messages. No attempt has been made to teach him Makaton signs or a symbol system.

Key policy principle

13

Planned restrictive physical interventions should be justified in respect of what is known of the service user from a formal multidisciplinary assessment, alternative approaches that have been tried, an evaluation of the potential risks involved and references to a body of expert knowledge and established good practice.

 Good practice

As part of a formal assessment, it was decided to observe Stephen's behaviour and record incidents that involved violence to others. This revealed that most of the time Stephen hits out with a single blow. Afterwards, he calms down quickly so long as other people do not try and get too close to him or discuss what he has 'done wrong'. Attempts at restrictive physical intervention immediately following an incident usually produce more serious and long-lasting aggressive behaviour. Practice guidelines for Stephen include:

- When Stephen hits out staff should keep at least five feet away from him and should not talk to him about the incident for a minimum of ten minutes and until he has calmed down.

- On some rare occasions Stephen does not calm down and has to be restrained. Stephen has Down's syndrome. This means he is likely to experience difficulties in breathing, especially if his chest is compressed or his mouth obstructed. It is also relatively easy for Stephen to dislocate bones in his neck. Staff have consulted Stephen's doctor and the physiotherapist about the method used to restrain him. Practice guidelines state that when any restrictive physical interventions are used, a service user should never be placed in a face-down position and no pressure should be applied to his neck or chest.

- Restrictive physical intervention has been used as an alternative to medication that was previously used. However, it was found that Stephen had a very high tolerance for the drugs that were being used and he required very high doses to achieve a noticeable effect on his behaviour. Stephen's doctor was involved in the decision to replace drugs with a programme that includes some restrictive physical interventions.

continued

Staff are confident that the approach they employ:

- is based on a detailed assessment of Stephen's behaviour
- incorporates measures to minimise the risks to Stephen
- reflects available expert knowledge and good practice
- is an improvement on the other approaches that have previously been tried

 Poor practice

Jane's attacks on her carers are extremely brief and can usually be stopped by reducing the demands being placed on Jane at the time. Carers feel that Jane is getting away without doing her fair share of household duties. The team agree that Jane must comply with their requests. They decide that if this results in attacks on them she will be restrained for a minimum of 15 minutes or until she calms down. One member of staff is an expert in martial arts and has agreed to train his colleagues in these methods of restraint. Unknown to the staff, Jane has a history of heart disease.

The importance of regular review

Restrictive physical interventions require regular review for a number of reasons:

- All restrictive physical interventions put the service user at risk of physical injury and psychological distress. A regular review is required to monitor possible side effects.

- Some people are particularly sensitive to certain kinds of sensory stimulation (eg touch), making the use of restrictive physical interventions even more problematic.

- Over time behaviour patterns will change as will the benefits and risks associated with any restrictive physical intervention. Each review should include a revised assessment of risk. (This is considered in more detail in Chapter 6.)

- Restrictive physical interventions should be combined with other approaches that lead towards the reduction or withdrawal of the restrictive physical intervention. Regular reviews should monitor progress towards this goal.

Key policy principle

14

The use of restrictive physical interventions should be subject to regular review.

 Good practice

Parmajit's care team obtained multidisciplinary approval to use restrictive physical interventions as part of a response plan devised two years ago. Major incidents have decreased dramatically due to the introduction of a package of preventative and positive strategies, but Parmajit still presents severe behavioural challenges from time to time. The restrictive physical intervention is reviewed every six weeks as part of Parmajit's care plan and more often if there are any difficulties (see Chapter 7). When necessary, the care plan and the procedures for responding to Parmajit's challenging behaviours are modified after each review. In addition to recording incidents of challenging behaviour, staff are encouraged to record events associated with Parmajit being calm or co-operative. This information is used to develop a comprehensive plan to address his challenging behaviour.

 Poor practice

Restrictive physical interventions were approved as a response strategy to help staff manage Gary's self-injurious behaviour eighteen months ago. It was anticipated that this would be required about twice per month on average. At that time, it was agreed that continued use of restrictive physical interventions would be subject to the analysis of incident records by a senior service manager and a clinical psychologist. Unfortunately, the manager left during the initial trial period and the first review never took place. Recording focuses solely on challenging behaviours and there is no attempt to interpret the information that has been collected. Staff continue to use these restrictive physical interventions about three times a week with Gary without any review.

Agenda for action

1. Are staff provided with written guidance on the permissible methods of restrictive physical intervention to be used with each service user?

2. For each service user who may experience some form of restrictive physical intervention, what strategies are in place to promote alternative, more appropriate forms of communication and behaviour?

3. Are restrictive physical interventions clearly justified in terms of the service user's previous history (including the range of alternative strategies that have been tried) and an up-to-date multidisciplinary assessment?

4. Is there a written summary of the reasons for using a particular restrictive physical intervention with each service user?

5. Do all service users who experience restrictive physical interventions receive regular routine reviews?

6. Are the results of sensory assessments used to inform discussions about the most appropriate way of responding to challenging behaviour?

7. Can additional reviews be triggered by changing circumstances surrounding the use of restrictive physical interventions?

Restrictive physical interventions and risk assessment

Evaluating risk

Almost every activity involves some element of risk. For example, a person making a cup of tea risks scalding themselves with hot water and someone who is careless when crossing the road could be hit by a car. Judgments about risk involve an assessment of the likelihood that adverse or unpleasant consequences will follow from our actions. This in turn is balanced against the benefits or positive outcomes that we expect to follow from our actions. In general, if we believe the risk of an unpleasant outcome is low in relation to the likelihood of a pleasant outcome we will probably accept the risk. For example, most people accept the low risk of being involved in a traffic accident in return for the many benefits that arise from driving a car.

The assessment of risk is complicated by our evaluation of the significance or impact of different outcomes. If the likely benefits from a course of action are seen to be very large we may be prepared to accept a very high level of risk. For example, many people are prepared to gamble on the National Lottery. The risk of losing money is very high but the potential benefits of winning are seen as making the risk worthwhile. On the other hand, if the negative outcome was very much more serious than losing a small amount of money we might be much more cautious in our assessment of risk. Consider, for example, the potential dangers associated with mountain climbing, bungee jumping or robbing a bank!

Risk assessment can be summarised as having three central components:

- the likelihood that actions will lead to positive or negative outcomes

- the relative size or significance of those outcomes

- actions that can reduce risk or mitigate the consequences of risk

Most people are reluctant to accept the risk of a life-threatening activity unless they believe the level of risk is very low. Air travel is accepted because people believe that the risk of a serious accident is very low. In contrast, activities that pose a high risk are often accepted if the negative outcome results in inconvenience rather than danger. Consider, for example, a summer holiday in Britain, driving above the speed limit on a motorway or visiting the theatre or cinema without first booking a seat. Figure 3 shows the level of perceived risk of adverse outcomes.

Figure 3 Level of perceived risk of adverse outcomes

Consequences	High risk	Low risk
High impact	Free-fall parachuting	Commercial air travel
Low impact	Buying a National Lottery ticket	Using a new recipe to make a cake

When a proposed course of action is associated with the risk of unwanted consequences, alternatives may be considered more attractive. In some circumstances there is the option of doing nothing. This might be completely safe (compared, for example to bungee jumping) because there is no risk of adverse outcomes. In other situations, there may be risks associated with every alternative course of action. Effective decisions will only be possible if the risks attached to each course of action are correctly evaluated. For example, consider the most appropriate actions for a bystander who is the only witness to a road traffic accident on a deserted road. Should the person help the accident victims or summon help?

Risk assessment and people who challenge services

Like anyone else, children and adults who use services will be exposed to varying degrees of risk. All service users are entitled to have their exposure to risk assessed. Services should take reasonable measures to reduce the level of risk especially where adverse consequences would have a significant impact on the service user's health or well-being. However, human rights and the values base described in Chapter 3 dictate that all service users should be able to make choices that influence their own lives. This includes the opportunity to make decisions that may result in adverse outcomes. Services are responsible for ensuring that such risks are reasonable. Every effort should be made to ensure that children and adults who use services are not exposed to unreasonable risk. This requires a structured approach to risk assessment.

The five steps for risk assessment

By law, the planning and delivery of services must include an assessment of risk for service users. The Health and Safety Executive has provided a framework for risk assessment that can be adapted for work with adults and children who present challenging behaviours. Procedures for risk assessment are designed to help staff:

1. identify activities or environments that are associated with risk

2. establish the likelihood of adverse outcomes for individual service users

3. estimate the consequences if such outcomes were to occur and take steps to avoid unreasonable risk

4. record all relevant information

5. undertake regular reviews

The five steps for risk assessment are illustrated with respect to the risks posed by John, a man who sometimes presents challenging behaviour:

John is a 23-year-old man with a severe learning disability and a diagnosis of autism. He shares a community house with six other adults, all of whom have severe learning disabilities. He has difficulty with all forms of communication and finds it extremely difficult to adjust to changes in his daily routines. Noise has been identified as an important setting condition (see Chapter 4) that often leads to aggression towards other people. When he is required to wait for activities he often becomes distressed and will sometimes engage in severe self-injurious behaviour such as punching his face or biting his wrists.

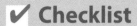 **Checklist**

John's risk assessment

Step 1   Look for hazards

For example:

- situations where John has to wait

- noisy environments

Step 2   Decide who might be harmed and how

For example:

- John – from self-injury

- staff – from aggression by John

The risks to John and to staff are:

- physical injury

- psychological distress arising from injury

- infection, particularly hepatitis

(Other service users have not been attacked.)

Step 3   Evaluate the risks arising from the hazards

Note whether these precautions are sufficient to control the risk
(either in terms of the likelihood of adverse outcomes or the severity
of the impact of adverse outcomes).

Existing measures include:

- training to ensure that staff understand the nature of
  John's difficulties with communication and his problems
  in adjusting to changes in routine

continued

- telling staff to avoid leaving John waiting for activities

- telling staff to make sure that John is not placed in noisy environments

- immunising staff and other service users against hepatitis B and tetanus
  (While the risk to other service users is, at present, low the adverse consequences of infection are considerable.)

Risks not managed include:

- new staff who do not help John to avoid the environmental setting conditions of 'waiting' and 'noise'

- other service users making unexpected noises that precipitate aggression

Step 4   Record findings

Measure the frequency, severity and duration of incidents that involve aggression or self-injury.

Setting conditions:

- noisy environments

- waiting

Action taken to reduce risk:

- ensuring that John does not spend long periods in noisy environments

- reducing the wait for activities to a minimum

Step 5   Review

- Reassess risk after one month.

- Explore strategies to help John cope more effectively with noisy environments and unavoidable periods of waiting (eg during mealtimes).

The assessment of risk in relation to the use of restrictive physical interventions

Since the use of restrictive physical interventions involves some level of risk for both staff and service users, it is essential that they are included in any risk assessment. Restrictive physical interventions that are deemed to present an unreasonable risk to service users, staff or members of the public should not be employed.

Key policy principle 15
Physical interventions should not involve unreasonable risk and potential hazards associated with the use of restrictive physical interventions should be systematically explored using a risk assessment procedure.

The factors that affect the degree of risk associated with restrictive physical interventions are set out in the following checklist.

✔ Checklist

Risk arising from the use of restrictive physical interventions

Step 1   Look for hazards

- What adverse outcomes could follow from the proposed restrictive physical intervention?

- What are the likely outcomes if no action is taken?

In some situations there may be a significant risk associated with doing nothing, and few potential hazards associated with taking decisive action. For example, a child who repeatedly grabs food from other people's plates at meal times may well end up being excluded from this kind of group activity.

continued

Holding the child's hands for a few minutes to prevent them taking food from other children is likely to pose few risks for an adult or the child concerned. Other incidents may require careful judgement to balance the relative risk of using a restrictive physical intervention compared with doing nothing. In all cases doing nothing is a realistic course of action that must be properly evaluated for risk.

Step 2   Decide who might be harmed and how

When restrictive physical interventions are used,
there are three groups of people who may be at risk:

- the service user whose behaviour is causing concern

- the staff who are directly involved in using a restrictive physical intervention

- other people in the vicinity, including other service users, other staff, visitors (to a service facility) and members of the public (if the incident occurs in a community setting)

An assessment of risk must consider the adverse outcomes for all three groups in relation to using a restrictive physical intervention and doing nothing.

Step 3   Evaluate the risks arising from the hazards

Note whether these precautions are sufficient to control the risk (either in terms of the likelihood of adverse outcomes or the severity of the impact of adverse outcomes).

The risk arising from the use of a restrictive physical intervention depends upon the precise nature of the procedures employed and the level of expertise owned by the staff who implement the procedure. Other things being equal, the level of risk to service users will be raised by interventions that:

continued

- rely upon the use of force

- are employed continuously over a period of time

- are employed frequently

- involve more than one member of staff

- are resisted by the service user

- are implemented by poorly trained staff

The risk to service users is minimised when the adverse consequences of challenging behaviours are controlled by the least restrictive effective physical intervention. This means that any restrictive physical intervention should be evaluated to control the risks posed by the service users' challenging behaviour by asking:

- What is the minimum force needed? (See Chapter 7)

- What is the minimum period of time needed? (See Chapter 7)

- What is the minimum frequency needed? (See Chapter 7)

- What is the minimum number of staff needed?

- What is the minimum level of staff training? (See Chapter 10)

Step 4   Record findings

Recording and monitoring the use of restrictive physical interventions is considered in Chapter 8.

Step 5   Review

The importance of regularly reviewing restrictive physical intervention procedures and their outcomes is considered in Chapters 5, 7 and 8.

A more problematic area of risk assessment concerns the evaluation of potential benefits that may be created by using restrictive physical interventions. Thus far, the assessment process has been concerned with weighing the potential risks arising from a restrictive physical intervention with the adverse consequences of challenging behaviours, such as aggression or self-injury. However, in some circumstances it might be argued that the risk associated with a restrictive physical intervention is justified, not by the reduction of risk from challenging behaviour, but by the creation of opportunities for a better quality of life for the service user.

For Russ and other people like him, quality of life is seriously affected by the occurrence of challenging behaviours. A person's current lifestyle can be seen in terms of the 'hazards' of missed opportunities for learning and the absence of new experiences. These 'hazards' can best be controlled by creating opportunities for the person to learn different ways of interacting with other people and a more varied pattern of daily activities. The use of a restrictive physical intervention is seen as necessary to create these learning opportunities. The risks associated with the restrictive physical intervention can be clearly identified and weighed against the long-term 'hazards' or risks associated with the person's current lifestyle.

 Good practice

Russ is a young man who has few social skills and becomes very agitated by any changes to his routine. When he first visits a new building or a room that has been rearranged he is likely to become distressed, making whining noises and banging his head with his fist and attacking other people.

In the past, this reaction to new surroundings significantly reduced Russ's quality of life as his carers were reluctant to take him anywhere new. He seldom left the house where he lived and only ever visited one corner shop. His interest in trains is restricted to repetitive games with a model railway he has had since childhood.

continued

Staff have now recognised that if they can help Russ to overcome his distress when confronted with a strange environment he very quickly settles down. The most effective method of doing this is for a member of staff to sit on either side of Russ and hold his arms firmly by his side. After two or three minutes Russ will relax and begin to look carefully at his surroundings. After another five minutes or so he is relaxed enough to wander around without physical contact although staff remain close by and offer reassurance through physical contact when necessary.

Following the introduction of this brief restrictive physical intervention, Russ has been able to visit a model railway, a transport museum and the local train station.

Poor practice

Denise travels to and from college by bus. She learned to cope with the long journey and all the noise made by the other passengers by listening to music on her MP3 player. One day some boys snatched the player from her and in the ensuing struggle it was broken. Without music to distract her Denise is easily upset by other people and the boys on the bus have learned that they can easily wind Denise up. She often gets into fights and is now regarded as disruptive. The bus driver has said that she must either be strapped into her seat so that she can't fight or he will ban her from using the bus.

The final aspect of risk assessment concerns the detrimental effects that follow if restrictive physical interventions are seen as long-term solutions to the management of challenging behaviour. This is particularly likely to happen where the procedure employed is perceived to be effective in addressing a challenging behaviour with a low level of risk to staff or service users. It is important to emphasise that restrictive physical interventions should only be used as temporary measures to ensure that service users are not exposed to unreasonable risk. Over time, alternative approaches should be introduced and service users should be able to participate in positive approaches to treatment and rehabilitation that render restrictive physical interventions unnecessary.

Agenda for action

1. What restrictive physical interventions are currently used or are sanctioned for use by members of staff?

2. What are the potential hazards associated with using each procedure?

3. Who is at risk when each restrictive physical intervention is used:

   - the service user who needs the intervention?

   - staff using the intervention?

   - other service users and members of staff?

   - members of the public?

4. What steps have been taken to minimise the likelihood that restrictive physical interventions will have adverse consequences for service users, staff and members of the public?

5. What is the least restrictive physical intervention that will enable staff to respond effectively to foreseeable incidents involving individual service users?

Minimising risks and promoting the well-being of service users

The general principle that restrictive physical interventions should be used to promote the best interests of service users was introduced in Chapter 2 on the legal framework. Chapter 5 considered how the concept of 'best interest' can be promoted by providing general guidance on individualised procedures, teaching service users alternative non-challenging behaviours and basing interventions on thorough multidisciplinary assessments. This chapter elaborates the concept of 'best interest' by introducing two additional considerations:

1. Every effort should be taken to minimise the risks associated with the use of restrictive physical interventions.

2. Interventions should, as far as possible, maintain and support the physical and psychological well-being of the service user.

These two principles are so closely linked that, in practice, they are complementary. Precautions that preserve and promote the well-being of clients are also likely to reduce risk. For this reason the development of policy on both topics is considered together.

Using reasonable force

'Reasonable force' involves two related concepts. Firstly, there is the question of whether the force used is proportionate to the desired outcome. For example, it is likely that a restrictive physical intervention used to prevent a young girl from scratching herself will be less forceful than the effort required to respond to a man who is violently attacking another person. Responses to violence and reckless behaviour should involve the application of the minimum level of force to prevent harm or minimise damage to property.

Secondly, the concept of reasonable force involves a consideration of whether other, less intrusive, actions could have been employed to achieve the same outcome. For example, if it is known that particular events have 'triggered' violence, a more appropriate response than restrictive physical interventions would be the removal of the environmental 'triggers'.

A practical application of the concept of minimum force is the 'gradient of control' (New York State Office of Mental Retardation and Developmental Disabilities, 1997). This procedure requires that when staff respond with a restrictive physical intervention, they follow a predetermined sequence that begins with the application of the least restrictive options and gradually increases the level of restriction. The sequence is terminated as soon as control is established over the person's behaviour.

Key policy principle 16   Restrictive physical interventions should be used with the minimum of reasonable force.

The gradient of support fits well with the concept of the 'assault cycle' (Rowett and Breakwell, 1992) that describes the typical stages of agitation and violence displayed by a person during an aggressive episode. It is proposed that low levels of force and less intrusive measures are likely to be effective early on in the cycle, while physical management may become the only option as the cycle proceeds. For example, attempts at defusion and distraction (see Chapter 4) should be made before employing defensive breakaway techniques and these should be introduced before using low-level restrictive physical interventions.

Good practice

Carers working with Jamila have learnt how to recognise early signs that her anxiety and agitation are building up to the point that severe self-injury and physical aggression are likely to occur. An early indicator is that Jamila starts pacing up and down and slapping the side of her body with her arm. If staff are unable to distract Jamila at this point, they know that she is likely to become aggressive and that restrictive physical interventions may be required. They have discovered that by placing a hand on her shoulder and then gently massaging her shoulder muscles they can help her to relax and calm down. Only staff trained in using the technique are permitted to work with her and it is always implemented when Jamila starts pacing and slapping her side. Consequently, restrictive physical interventions are seldom required.

 Poor practice

Nicky screams several times a day. Occasionally these screams are followed by attempts to punch staff. Whenever Nicky screams, three staff physically restrain him as a precautionary measure. These episodes are not recorded by staff and there is no programme to reduce the incidents using active procedures.

Using interventions for the shortest period of time

Whenever restrictive physical interventions are used, a central concern should be to return personal control of their actions to the person concerned as quickly as possible. In practice, this means that as the person calms and regains their composure, the level of restriction applied through physical interventions should be systematically reduced. Rather than removing all forms of intervention at the same time, it may be helpful to use the 'gradient of support' in reverse. For example, Willis and Lavigna (1985) provide the following guidelines for disengaging a physical intervention.

Key policy principle 17 Any single application of restrictive physical intervention should be used for the minimum period of time consistent with the best interests of the service user.

✔ Checklist

Removing physical intervention

1   Gradually lessen muscle tension.

2   Gradually reduce the intensity of the containment contact (eg instead of holding arms around the person, move to one side and hold both their hands; then hold only one hand).

3   Gradually move from a physical intervention to shadowing (eg instead of holding a person, rest a hand on them).

4   Increase the space available by moving away from them.

5   Gradually decrease the number of staff involved.

6   As the person appears to become more composed, ask them 'Are you OK?', 'Are you feeling better?' or 'Are you calm now?'

(Based on Willis and Lavigna, 1985)

  Good practice

Staff working with Jed have worked out the usual pattern of his aggressive outbursts. They know that Jed likes to have two people hold his hands when he gets upset and begins to lose control. Staff keep talking to Jed even when he is shouting and swearing. Eventually, he calms down and will tell staff when he wants them to let go of his hands. At this point, one member of staff leaves while the other stays with Jed, talking to him and holding both his hands if Jed asks them to.

Poor practice

A service policy states that whenever restraint is required it should last for a minimum of 15 minutes and involve at least three members of staff to ensure compliance.

Key policy principle 18 The use of restrictive physical interventions should be sanctioned for the shortest period of time consistent with the individual service user's best interests.

Restrictive physical interventions should be viewed as short-term measures. They should always be accompanied by plans that set out what steps need to be taken to minimise their role in the management of challenging behaviours. There should be a clearly established timescale for reviewing the use of restrictive physical interventions with each service user. Immediate review of the person's behaviour and the use of restrictive physical intervention should take place in the event of any of the developments shown in the following checklist.

✔ **Checklist**

Emergency review of restrictive physical interventions

1   Restrictive physical interventions are used more frequently than had been anticipated.

2   Restrictive physical interventions are used with increasing frequency over time.

continued

3   Staff report that the agreed procedures do not enable them to control the person's behaviour.

4   Injuries occur to the person receiving the intervention.

5   Injuries occur to staff involved in using restrictive physical interventions.

6   Interventions do not appear to be employed according to the agreed procedures.

7   New challenging behaviours develop (other than those initially identified) that may also require the use of restrictive physical interventions.

 Good practice

In a house for people with challenging behaviour and mental illness, the service manager reviews the frequency with which restrictive physical interventions are used on a monthly basis. No procedure is sanctioned for use for more than three months at a time. If restrictive physical intervention is required more than twice in any 30-day period for any service user, the person's care planning team meets to consider each incident and decide what additional measures, including preventative strategies, may be required. The revised plan is submitted to the service's ethics committee which has overall responsibility for any use of restrictive physical interventions.

 Poor practice

In another house for people with challenging behaviour and mental illness, once it is has been decided that restrictive physical interventions may have to be used with a service user, that person's file is marked with a yellow sticker. The agreements are seldom reviewed and the stickers are never removed irrespective of any changes in the service user's behaviour.

Minimising discomfort

Some methods of restrictive physical intervention involve the application of localised pressure in the form of thumb, wrist or arm 'locks'. The level of discomfort and pain experienced by the service user can be increased or decreased by varying the amount of pressure used in the 'lock'. The extent to which pain is inflicted is directly related to the efficacy of the immobilisation procedure (McDonnell et al, 1993).

There are a number of compelling arguments to support the recommendation that techniques that subject service users to discomfort and pain should not be used:

- These techniques were developed to control groups of people who present different needs and challenges from those with learning disabilities (McDonnell et al, 1991).

- Since other methods that do not involve pain and discomfort are available, it is extremely doubtful whether techniques based upon the infliction of pain can meet the criterion of 'minimum force'.

- Methods that do not reflect the application of 'minimum force' could not easily be defended in a court of law.

- Techniques that involve pain carry considerable risk of injury to the service user.

- There is some evidence to suggest that management techniques that involve elements of aggression may increase rather than decrease the level of aggression presented by the service user (Donellan et al, 1988).

There are other forms of restrictive physical intervention that are effective with people with a learning disability and do not involve inflicting pain (New York State Office of Mental Retardation and Developmental Disabilities 1988 and 1997, revised version).

Key policy Restrictive physical interventions
principle should not cause pain.

19

Good practice

Nolde School provides care and education for children who display high levels of aggression and self-injury. Staff use a variety of restrictive physical interventions that are carefully designed to avoid pain or discomfort for the pupils. For example, one older pupil is sometimes placed in a chair so that two staff can use enough of their body weight on his forearms to limit movement and thereby prevent self-injury. No pressure is applied to his joints. The staff believe that using a chair is a more socially acceptable method than applying a restrictive physical intervention to someone lying on the floor (McDonnell et al, 1991; 1993).

 Poor practice

Staff working with a group of adolescents who display high levels of aggression are concerned about two young men who sometimes throw wild punches. Although there have never been any serious injuries, the staff have been trained by a self-defence expert who usually runs self-defence courses for members of the public concerned about attacks by muggers. The training involves identifying weak points on an aggressor's body and escaping from attacks by using finger jabs and punches to vulnerable areas.

Individual assessment

People with learning disabilities are at a significantly greater risk of experiencing a wide range of medical complications compared to other members of the population (Welsh Health Planning Forum, 1992; Department of Health, 1995). There are a number of medical conditions that increase the risk of serious injury if restrictive physical interventions are used. Where these risk factors are present it is important that medical advice is sought before any intervention is approved. In addition, there are a number of complications that may arise while a restrictive physical intervention is being employed. In this event, the intervention should be terminated immediately and medical assistance summoned. Similarly, if there are any concerns about a person's health after a restrictive physical intervention has been employed, medical help should be obtained without delay.

✔ Checklist

Contraindications of restrictive physical interventions

1 Take medical advice on the use of restrictive physical interventions if the service user:

- has a history of heart disease or heart problems

- has difficulty in breathing or a history of respiratory illness

- has problems with digesting food or gastro-intestinal conditions

- has recent fractures or a history of dislocated joints

- has Down's syndrome

- is an older person

2 Terminate restrictive physical interventions immediately if the person shows signs of:

- breathing difficulties; very rapid breathing

- fits or seizures

- vomiting

- blue coloration of hands, feet or other body parts (indicates reduced blood circulation)

- mottling (paleness/yellowing of skin due to restricted blood circulation)

- bone fractures

(New York Office of Mental Retardation and Developmental Disabilities, SCIP, 1988)

Key policy principle 20 Service users should have individual assessments to identify contraindications to restrictive physical interventions before they are approved.

 Good practice

After a multidisciplinary team discussion, the medical consultant and physiotherapist provide a written statement to confirm that there are no unacceptable health risks associated with a planned restrictive physical intervention for a particular person with Down's syndrome. It is agreed to review this statement on a six-monthly basis to ensure it remains appropriate.

 Poor practice

Restrictive physical intervention is used several times a month for Tanya. The intervention involves two members of staff holding Tanya on the floor while she struggles, bites and kicks. This sometimes lasts for half an hour. Tanya gets very distressed and is often short of breath for several minutes. The manager has ruled out asking for medical advice and claims that Tanya exaggerates her distress 'just to make a fuss'.

Whenever a restrictive physical intervention is used there is an increased risk of physical injury or serious psychological distress for the service user concerned. The way in which staff respond to the person following the use of a restrictive physical intervention will have a number of important implications. For example, the management of the post-intervention period is likely to affect:

- the psychological well-being of the service user

- the likelihood that the person will present similar extreme forms of challenging behaviour in future

- the relationship between the service user and the staff

- the relationship between the staff and their manager(s)

For this reason, it is important to ensure that the service users do not experience any lasting adverse effects. They should be checked by a third person for any minor injuries such as scratches, abrasions and bruises, and if these have occurred they should be treated and the injuries recorded. In addition, the person should be given support and encouragement to talk through what happened and to re-establish their regular activities and routines. Staff should not blame the service user or create anxiety by reminding them of the adverse consequences if there is a recurrence of the challenging behaviour. Following a risk assessment, positive efforts should be made by staff to reintegrate the person in social settings at the earliest opportunity and to help them to restore relationships with friends and colleagues.

Key policy principle 21 Service users who received a restrictive physical intervention should be routinely assessed for signs of injury or psychological distress.

Good practice

Following advice from the local special support team, staff in a social education centre adopt the following procedures after any incident that requires a restrictive physical intervention:

1. The service user is given time and a safe place to recover their composure.

2. The person's key worker comes to talk to them about what happened and about their feelings after the incident.

3. A doctor is called in the event of any signs of physical distress or injury.

4. A risk assessment is undertaken to explore potential hazards and a risk management plan is agreed.

5. The key worker supports the person in rejoining group activities.

6. The person is not expected to apologise or justify their actions.

 Poor practice

Staff in a special school are trying to contain a young man for the last few remaining weeks before the end of the school term when he will transfer to a social services day centre. None of the staff want to take responsibility for Malcolm and when he becomes aggressive the male members of staff are always called in to 'handle him'. After Malcolm has calmed down, he is made to return to his classroom and apologise to the teacher for being 'naughty'. He then has to sit on a special seat and is not allowed to join in with other classroom activities. The staff constantly tell him that if he misbehaves after he leaves school he will be sent away to a special place for 'really bad boys'.

Agenda for action

1.   What steps have been taken to ensure that all instances of restrictive physical intervention are employed with the minimum of reasonable force?

2.   How are restrictive physical interventions monitored to ensure that any single intervention is applied for the shortest period of time consistent with the service user's best interest?

3.   How often are service users who receive restrictive physical interventions reviewed and what procedures are in place to ensure that alternative approaches (that do not involve restrictive physical interventions) are thoroughly explored?

4.   What steps have been taken to ensure that the restrictive physical interventions used do not cause pain?

5.   What steps have been taken to assess or reassess potential hazards and manage risk?

6.   How are service users assessed for possible contraindications before restrictive physical interventions are approved?

7.   Are service users who are exposed to restrictive physical interventions routinely assessed for signs of distress immediately following an incident and what steps are taken if there is evidence of distress or injury?

Chapter 8

Management responsibilities

Provision of care

Service managers have a number of major responsibilities relating to the provision of care. Firstly, managers are responsible for ensuring that care staff act in ways that are within the law and consistent with the organisation's values and principles (see Chapters 2 and 3). It should never be assumed that individual members of staff will have a detailed knowledge of the law or that they will share the organisation's values. Managers should guard against the possibility that within an organisation a group culture develops that is out of step with the values and aims expressed centrally.

Secondly, managers should ensure that the needs of service users are properly met (see Chapter 3). Any decision to use a restrictive physical intervention should involve careful consideration of the best interests of the service user (see Chapters 5 and 7).

Thirdly, managers have responsibility for safety in the workplace (Health and Safety at Work Act 1974). Service users who present challenging behaviours are likely to increase the risk of injury for themselves, other service users and staff. Restrictive physical interventions should be designed to minimise the risk of injury arising from challenging behaviour (see Chapters 6 and 7). It is also essential that the physical intervention itself does not increase the risk of injury to the person who receives the intervention or to the staff who apply it.

Incidents of challenging behaviour that provoke unplanned or emergency responses from staff are associated with higher levels of risk (Spreat et al, 1986; Hill and Spreat, 1987). Managers, therefore, have a responsibility to minimise the number of occasions on which service users who challenge are exposed to unplanned forms of restraint. Wherever possible, managers should seek to establish clear guidance on how staff should respond to the specific challenges presented by individual service users (see Chapter 5).

Managers will be able to meet these responsibilities with greater confidence if there is a clear written policy on the use of restrictive physical interventions and written guidance on the way in which restrictive physical interventions are to be used with individual service users.

Other chapters of this book provide detailed guidance on the scope and content of a policy. This chapter considers policy development and implementation, guidance on the use of specific restrictive physical interventions, monitoring and recording, complaints procedures, and resource management.

Implementing policies

A number of management strategies can help with implementation. These are set out in the following checklist.

✔ Checklist

Policy implementation

1   All staff and service users should be involved in the development of policy statements.

Consultation will build confidence and reduce anxiety about any proposed changes to established work practices. Circulate draft documents widely and encourage comment.

2   The policy should be written in clear, simple prose that can be easily understood. Provide staff and service users with training opportunities to ensure that everyone understands what the policy says and how it affects day-to-day relationships between staff and service users.

3   Each member of staff should receive a copy of the final policy. It may be helpful to ask everyone to sign to show that they have received a copy. Newly appointed staff should receive a copy as part of their induction training.

continued

4   Induction training should include key principles of restrictive physical interventions and a practical introduction by a registered trainer.

5   Regular training updates should be provided for all staff and service users by an accredited trainer with expertise in body mechanics and safety. The content and frequency will depend on the nature of the service and the extent to which restrictive physical interventions are used.

6   Monitoring of staff performance and supervisory discussions should include reference to incidents and events covered by the policy.

7   The policy should be reviewed at least annually and amended in the light of experience. Feedback from staff and service users should contribute to the review process.

8   Other organisations that provide services for the people who present a challenge should be made aware of the policy and invited to consider the development of a co-ordinated approach to restrictive physical interventions.

9   The parents and other family members and advocates of service users who may require restrictive physical interventions should be consulted and invited to comment on the policy.

Key policy principle

22   Service managers are responsible for developing and implementing policies on the use of restrictive physical interventions.

Guidance on the use of specific procedures

A policy provides a general framework of values, attitudes and expectations to assist staff in making appropriate judgments about their actions in relation to service users. Where it is known that the challenges presented by particular service users are likely to require some form of restrictive physical intervention, managers have a responsibility to work with staff to establish a planned response. This will involve guidance on the procedures that should be used with individual service users. Guidance on specific procedures must be consistent with the statements set out in the policy.

Compared to emergency or unplanned reactions to challenging behaviours, planned responses cause less distress and discomfort to the service user. They also result in fewer injuries to both staff and service users (see Chapter 4).

Key policy principle 23   The use of any restrictive physical intervention should be clearly set out in the form of written guidance for staff.

The information that should be included in guidance and provided to all staff who are authorised to employ restrictive physical interventions is set out in the following checklist.

✔ Checklist

Information for staff authorised to use restrictive physical interventions

1. the name of the service user

2. the behaviours that may require the use of the restrictive physical intervention procedure

3. the specific procedure to be used and the maximum duration of any single application

4. the names of specific staff who have been trained to use the procedure

5. the circumstances when the procedure may be used

6. the role of each member of staff during the incident (eg who should summon help and who should take responsibility for other service users)

7. how and when the restrictive physical intervention should be terminated

8. how the person who received the intervention should be treated afterwards and the steps needed to establish relations with staff and other service users

9. when and how the incident should be reported to an authority external to the organisation

Good practice

Bobby has autism and severe learning disabilities. He does not speak and is anxious, withdrawn and fearful of people. Often he tries to run away or climb on furniture, cars or buildings. This behaviour is considered to place him at considerable risk of injury.

Together, his mother and the staff at his school worked out a programme to teach him to stay close to adults during intervals between properly supervised activities. This involved the use of reins to physically prevent him from running away or climbing. The procedure for using the reins was written down. This described which adults were involved, the situations when the reins were to be used, how long they could be used for, what Bobby should be encouraged to do while he was wearing the reins, and a system for recording how often the reins were used and how Bobby reacted. This information was circulated to Bobby's parents, the local education authority and the social services department with a written request for approval.

Following the introduction of the programme, there was an immediate improvement in Bobby's behaviour. Staff commented that he seemed relieved that other people were helping him to manage a behaviour he could not deal with on his own. After three months, staff felt confident that he no longer needed the reins. When the reins were removed, he stayed close to staff and did not try to run away.

 Poor practice

Leon has always presented violent behaviour especially when he is asked to do anything different. Staff routinely tie Leon into a chair to have his lunch and he always wears a specially designed jacket with sleeves tied together so that the movement of his arms is restricted. There is no documentation to indicate how this approach should be used, which staff should be involved or what it is intended to achieve. No one seems to be responsible for reviewing Leon's situation.

Key policy principle 24 Service managers are responsible for ensuring that all incidents that involve the use of a restrictive physical intervention are clearly, comprehensively and promptly recorded.

Honest and accurate recording by staff provides a permanent recording of the events surrounding the use of restrictive physical interventions. This has a number of advantages:

- It will help to improve the quality of services for people with challenging behaviour.

- It will help prevent inappropriate treatment of service users.

- It provides protection for staff who may be required to give a detailed account of their actions.

- It assists in monitoring the implementation of policy and the use of agreed procedures.

- It will indicate the need for management action in response to the use of unplanned or emergency restrictive physical interventions.

- It is an integral part of a risk assessment procedure (see Chapter 6).

Recording will not occur unless staff are convinced that it leads to positive practical outcomes. It is therefore important to provide staff on a regular basis with clear feedback using summary data from their records. Managers are responsible for ensuring that the workloads of individual members of staff permit recording to take place.

What should be recorded?

The minimum information that should be recorded each time a restrictive physical intervention is employed as a way of managing violent or aggressive behavior is summarised in the following checklist.

✔ Checklist

What to record after using a restrictive physical intervention

1   the date, time and location of the incident

2   the names of the staff and service users involved

3   the names of all those who witnessed the events

4   who was informed – managers, parents, doctors, regulators

5   a description of the events leading up to the incident

6   details of any variation from the individual care plan leading up to the incident

7   the interventions used and their duration

8   a description of how the incident was resolved

9   injuries to staff or service users

10   damage to property or possessions

11   physical and psychological effects of the restrictive physical intervention on the service user

12   additional action taken or recommended

13   the date of the record

14   the name of the person completing the record and their signature

Staff should be given clear instructions about when to record, how to record (the kind of language and the format) and when to report to management. Arrangements should be made to store records safely and to protect the confidentiality of those concerned. The records should be made available on request to all authorised personnel visiting the establishment. Managers are responsible for regularly reviewing staff records to ensure that staff:

- adhere to policies

- understand the causes of challenging behaviours presented by individual service users

- monitor agreed procedures

- initiate review meetings in the case of unplanned restrictive physical interventions

 Good practice

Selina chews her fingers so badly that staff have agreed to use arm splints to prevent further tissue damage. One member of staff on each shift in her hostel is responsible for monitoring her behaviour, deciding whether the splints are required, supervising the placement of the splints on her arms, regular observation while she wears the splints, deciding when the splints can be removed and the completion of a detailed record using a pro forma sheet.

 Poor practice

Tina is a young woman with a profound learning disability who occasionally grabs and pulls other people's hair. At other times she enjoys watching pop videos. She lives in a house with five other people with learning disabilities. The following report was filed by one of Tina's carers following an incident of severe challenging behaviour:

Yesterday Tina was in a bad mood for no apparent reason. She was continually trying to pull everyone's hair. She was told not to do it several times. Eventually, I shouted at her and said, 'Go to your room'. Tina pulled my hair so I pulled hers back. I removed her hands from my hair and she spat at me so I spat back. To cut a long story short, I ended up holding her on the floor using the restraint we have been told to use.

continued

It should be apparent that this report is unclear and unsatisfactory for a number of reasons:

- It is not dated and no times are given.

- There is no information about events leading up to Tina's hair pulling.

- There is no information about other members of staff.

- There is no information about other service users.

- It is not clear whether the staff response was part of an agreed procedure. (If it is not part of an agreed procedure, it probably constitutes an assault.)

- The account of what happened is incomplete – 'to cut a long story short' is not acceptable.

- The description of the physical intervention is unclear and incomplete.

- It is not clear how long the incident lasted or how it was resolved.

Involving service users

In addition to being consulted when policies are being prepared or reviewed, service users have a right to be involved in monitoring good practice. This can be achieved in a number of ways including providing the opportunity for service users' committees or forums to discuss the use of restrictive physical interventions. An important mechanism to safeguard the interests of service users is an effective complaints procedure.

Key policy principle 25 All service users and their families and representatives should have ready access to an effective complaints system.

Effective complaints systems have three important characteristics:

- a mechanism that permits managers to respond promptly and to deal with complaints as and when they arise

- access to external and independent adjudicators to consider serious incidents or to investigate complaints that cannot be satisfactorily resolved by service managers

- a safe environment where service users feel free to express complaints without fear of subsequent recriminations by staff or other service users

Where service users are unable to participate in monitoring good practice and issuing complaints, advocates should be asked to represent them. It is essential that advocates are carefully selected, trained and supported and that they act completely independently of the service provider.

Whistleblowing

Employers and managers have a responsibility to ensure that policies that require staff to draw attention to abusive, poor or otherwise unacceptable practice are in place. Such action is known as 'whistleblowing'.

All staff should understand that if they fail to report poor practice they will share responsibility for what has occurred and could face disciplinary action. Staff should be reassured that whistleblowers will be fully supported and protected from retaliation or discrimination by colleagues or other staff.

Managers are responsible for creating a climate of trust and ensuring that all staff receive training and support on whistleblowing. The way in which the service supports whistleblowing should be fully documented using formats that are easily accessible by all members of staff.

The central features of an effective complaints procedure are set out in the following checklist.

✔ **Checklist**

A complaints procedure

1 The scope and remit of the complaints procedure is clearly defined.

2 The system is easy for service users or their representatives to access.

3 There are clear timescales for each stage of the procedure.

4 There is a system for appeal to trusted and respected individuals who are independent of the provider agency.

5 The outcome of any investigation is communicated to all concerned and recommendations are promptly implemented.

6 Staff will need to have confidence in the impartiality and effectiveness of the complaints system if they are to promote rather than frustrate its use.

 Good practice

Leroy's mother became concerned about bruises on his arms and legs after he had spent a couple of days receiving respite care. After a call to the social worker in charge, she was visited by another member of the social services who made detailed notes about her concerns. Within ten days she was told that her complaint had led to a disciplinary hearing in respect of one junior member of staff. A month later she received another letter saying that following her complaint the member of staff responsible for Leroy's injuries had been dismissed for inappropriate use of a restrictive physical intervention. The social worker in charge apologised for the distress that the incident may have caused her and Leroy and asked her to visit the respite home to discuss any outstanding concerns.

Poor practice

Zoe's brother became concerned after her behaviour towards him and other men suddenly changed shortly after she moved into a new group home. Gerry phoned the home but wasn't able to speak to anyone in authority. When he tried to contact the voluntary organisation that was providing care for Zoe, no one seemed to know who was responsible for dealing with complaints. Eventually, he spoke to an administrative assistant who said she would pass his message on. After five weeks and further phone calls he received a short note saying that Zoe had settled in and was making lots of friends. There was no reference to his concern about her changed behaviour.

Resource management

The most important resource available to managers is experienced and skilled staff. Staff shortages, low staff morale or the limited competencies of existing staff are frequently put forward by way of explanation for service deficits. Staff shortages due to sickness or recruitment delays are sometimes unavoidable, and it may be difficult to obtain competent temporary cover no matter how willing the organisation is to fund it. Such circumstances may lead to an increase in the level of challenging behaviour presented by service users and, consequently, an increased use of restrictive physical interventions.

When short-term cover is used, managers will need to brief relief staff on the policy with respect to restrictive physical interventions and ensure that they know how to implement approved management strategies with individual service users. Managers may also consider increasing the level of support and supervision available to temporary staff.

Long-term staff shortages and gaps in expertise that result from the inappropriate use of financial resources are unacceptable. Such practices are likely to render the organisation subject to legal proceedings in the event of injuries to staff or service users that arise from inadequate levels of staffing or staff being required to undertake duties for which they have not been properly trained.

Key policy principle 26   Careful consideration should be given to the impact of resource management on the use of restrictive physical interventions.

Managers should ask whether staffing levels or staff competencies contribute to:

- the frequency with which restrictive physical interventions are employed

- the number of unplanned restrictive physical interventions

- the number of injuries sustained as a consequence of using restrictive physical interventions

Where staff shortages arising from poor resource management are having an adverse impact on the management of challenging behaviours, managers have a responsibility to bring this to the attention of their senior colleagues.

 Good practice

The manager of a group home for people with severe learning disabilities became increasingly concerned about the level of minor aggression and property damage presented by three young men. She suspected that the underlying cause was increasing boredom following a cut in staffing. Previously, the three men had been able to go into the local town, to shop, visit the snooker hall and drink in pubs. Now they were expected to spend most days watching television. The manager prepared a formal report documenting the increasing number of challenging incidents after the staff cut and expressing her view that this was significantly affecting the quality of life for everyone in the home. Within two weeks, two additional staff were allocated to work specifically with the three young men.

Poor practice

Ahmed was recently resettled from a local authority hostel to a small house in the local community. Sometimes Ahmed wakes in the night and if he is not supervised he sometimes wanders out of the house. He was given a bedroom next to the room used for the sleeping night staff, but because of fears that he could fall down the stairs if he came out of his bedroom at night staff adopted the practice of locking the bedroom door when he was asleep. Staff argued that he could not be given a bedroom on the ground floor because the staff would not hear him if he got out of bed. Eventually the situation was resolved when the authority agreed to pay for a member of staff on night waking watch.

Agenda for action

1. Is there a policy to guide you and any staff for whom you are responsible in the use of restrictive physical interventions?

2. Are you and any staff for whom you are responsible fully conversant with the contents of the policy relating to the use of restrictive physical interventions?

3. Have staff and service users, parents and advocates, been consulted on the contents of the policy?

4. Have other organisations that share responsibility for providing services for people who challenge been consulted?

5. Are there written guidelines for practice that describe the use of specific restrictive physical interventions with individual service users and are fully consistent with the policy relating to the use of restrictive physical interventions?

6. What methods are used to record the use of restrictive physical interventions? How is this information used to improve practice?

7. How do service users, their families and representatives use the complaints procedure?

8. How does the management of resources within the organisation affect the use of restrictive physical interventions and how can it be improved?

Chapter 9

Employers' responsibilities to staff

Employers have a statutory responsibility to protect the health and safety of members of staff. When a job involves activities that could result in personal injury or high levels of stress, employers are required to evaluate and minimise the level of risk. Employers are responsible for ensuring that staff are not exposed to unreasonable risk while at work (see Chapter 2 and Health and Safety Executive, 1994).

Notwithstanding the routine risks of working with people who present challenging behaviours, staff who are required to use restrictive physical interventions are exposed to two additional kinds of risk:

- They may experience injury or psychological distress as a direct result of applying a restrictive physical intervention, especially if this happens frequently.

- Without appropriate safeguards, any use of restrictive physical interventions may be in breach of the law so that staff are at risk of criminal or civil proceedings (see Chapter 2).

Employers and managers are responsible for ensuring that restrictive physical interventions are applied in ways that minimise the risks to staff. This is most effectively achieved through the development of a clear and coherent policy (see Chapters 5 and 8).

Preventing injury and stress to employees

Organisational policy statements should make it clear that restrictive physical interventions should not put staff at risk of injury. When injuries do occur, staff are entitled to appropriate medical treatment and sick leave. Staff exposed to violent incidents or the repeated use of restrictive physical interventions may become distressed. Procedures should be in place to monitor staff stress arising from the use of restrictive physical interventions. All staff should have access to ongoing supervision and, where appropriate, professional counselling. It is known that staff respond to physical danger and psychological stress in different ways. Support following incidents of violence or aggression should reflect the individual needs and strengths of different members of staff.

Key policy principle

27

Employers and managers are responsible for the safety and well-being of staff.

 Good practice

The policy statement at Pinetree School clearly states that staff should not expose themselves to unreasonable risk of injury when working with people who are violent or aggressive. Procedures for using restrictive physical intervention are clearly explained and staff receive practical training. Whenever staff are injured, they are provided with medical treatment immediately after the incident. On the advice of the medical practitioner, staff are provided with sick leave to recover from injury. Review of restrictive physical intervention procedures is a routine feature of staff supervisions. Whenever it is suspected that a member of staff is experiencing stress as a consequence of challenging behaviours, they are required to meet with an experienced counsellor and, if necessary, take sick leave.

Poor practice

At Willow Wood School, injuries to staff are tolerated as being an inevitable consequence of using restrictive physical interventions. Staff are asked to work with people who are known to be violent but are not given training in how they should respond if attacked. Seeking medical treatment or counselling is seen by staff and managers as a sign of weakness and an inability to cope with the demands of the job. Injuries are seen as a reflection of incompetence and staff are not expected to take sick leave.

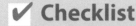 **Checklist**

Protecting staff through the policy on restrictive physical interventions

1   How does the policy seek to minimise injuries to staff who use restrictive physical interventions?

2   What procedures are in place for supporting staff with injuries when they occur?

3   How do staff apply for sick leave if they are injured?

4   How would managers or supervisors know if a member of staff was under stress as a result of challenging behaviour?

5   Are staff encouraged to discuss their own reactions to using restrictive physical interventions during supervision meetings?

6   Are counselling services available to staff who regularly work with people who present severe challenging behaviour?

Key policy principle 28

All restrictive physical interventions and any associated incidents that give cause for concern must be recorded and reported.

Staff should be clear about how restrictive physical interventions are to be carried out and what they are expected to achieve. They also need to know how each procedure reflects the organisation's policy on restrictive physical interventions. Staff should be given frequent opportunities to discuss the way in which restrictive physical interventions are carried out and to what extent they are effective. They need to know how to register a complaint about the use of restrictive physical interventions and what actions should follow (see Chapter 8). All complaints should be thoroughly investigated. Staff should never be penalised for expressing concerns about the use of restrictive physical interventions. Records of restrictive physical interventions may be inspected by the Commission for Social Care Inspection.

✔ Checklist

How staff should monitor good practice

1   What opportunities are available to groups of staff for talking about the use of restrictive physical interventions?

2   Are staff asked during supervision meetings to comment on the way in which restrictive physical interventions are planned and implemented?

3   What happens if a member of staff expresses concern about the way in which restrictive physical interventions are employed?

4   What should staff do if they wish to make a formal complaint?

5   What are the consequences for a member of staff who makes a formal complaint?

6   Are staff aware of the implications of child protection and protection of vulnerable adults (POVA) procedures for any use of restrictive physical interventions?

Good practice

Staff receive regular briefings on the restrictive physical interventions that are currently being employed. At team meetings the interventions are reviewed and discussed in the light of the organisational policy on restrictive physical interventions. Staff are expected to comment on the use of restrictive physical interventions when they meet their supervisor. Any concerns raised by staff are documented and followed up. Specific complaints about inappropriate ways of working with service users trigger an automatic formal inquiry.

 Poor practice

Staff rarely discuss the restrictive physical interventions that are employed. Discussion of the methods that other members of staff use to manage challenging behaviours is seen as unprofessional meddling. When one member of staff expressed concerns to her manager she was told not to interfere with things she didn't understand. There is no system for dealing with formal complaints.

Training staff to use restrictive physical interventions is covered in more detail in Chapter 10.

Agenda for action

1. Is the employer's responsibility for staff safety and well-being described in the policy document?

2. What are staff entitlements in the event of injury or psychological distress arising from the use of restrictive physical interventions?

3. How are staff encouraged to monitor good practice and report incidents that involve poor practice?

Chapter 10
Staff training

What training should cover

The effectiveness of any policy will ultimately depend on the success with which it is implemented by staff. Successful implementation will depend on staff knowing the contents of the policy document and having the knowledge and skills to put this into action. Training will therefore need to address:

- the policy on restrictive physical interventions

- the skills and knowledge required for implementation

- procedures to ensure that staff training meets appropriate standards

This chapter considers the way in which organisational policies can promote effective staff training.

Key policy principle 29 Staff who may be required to use restrictive physical interventions should receive regular training on knowledge, skills and values.

Training should make explicit reference to the values that underpin work with people with learning disabilities (see Chapter 3) and the ways of using restrictive physical interventions without compromising these principles. It should provide comprehensive and detailed coverage of the organisation's policy in relation to restrictive physical interventions and practical training on work with adults and/or children who challenge services. A more detailed summary of the practical topics that should be covered in staff training is provided in the following checklist.

✔ Checklist

Key topics for staff training

1   Maintaining positive values while working with people who challenge

2   Legal responsibilities and protection for people who use services

3   The contents of the employer organisation's policy on restrictive physical interventions

4   Strategies for primary prevention

5   Strategies for secondary prevention

6   Developing appropriate behaviours, using positive support and person-centred planning

7   How to use restrictive physical interventions approved by the employer organisation

8   How to implement the principles of:

- least restrictive physical intervention

- gradient of support

9   Teamwork and collaboration with other professionals

10   Record keeping and reporting

NB This is a guide to assist service providers and trainers. The contents of any training programme should be designed to meet the needs of service users and staff in each situation where training is provided.

Good practice

New Homes is a local independent provider of small group homes for people with a learning disability. Two of their homes are designed to be used by people with challenging behaviour. The organisation has a general policy on working with people with a learning disability. One section is specifically concerned with people who challenge. The team leader is responsible for making sure that all staff understand and conform to the policies relating to people who challenge. In-house training is provided every six months on practical methods of working with people who challenge. There are regular reviews of support strategies that are recorded and shared with all relevant staff.

 Poor practice

Leabank is a small private residential school for pupils with severe learning disabilities. Over the years the number of pupils who present 'problem behaviour' has grown. The owners of the school feel that too much emphasis on these 'problem' children will discourage local authorities from using the school. As a result, issues around behaviour management are never discussed. All the money from the training budget is spent on making sure that the teaching staff are up to date with the National Curriculum.

Choosing the right trainer and training programme

Trainers should have extensive experience of working with adults and children with severe learning disabilities who present challenging behaviours. They should have a detailed practical knowledge of restrictive physical interventions and be conversant with the principles for using restrictive physical interventions that are set out in other parts of this book. Their approach should reflect the values base set out in Chapter 2.

While there are many professionals who offer training in the use of restrictive physical interventions, not all would use methods that reflect these principles. Poor or ineffective training can undermine staff morale and increase the level of risk to both staff and service users. Anyone wishing to engage a training consultant should therefore exercise extreme caution and make extensive enquiries about the trainer's experience, the approaches they adopt and the quality of the training they provide.

Key policy principle

30

Training should be provided by a trainer with appropriate experience and qualifications.

The following checklist is offered as a guide to the questions that may be used when choosing a person to undertake staff training.

✔ Checklist

What makes a good trainer?

1   Does the trainer emphasise the rights of service users and the importance of training to be set within a framework of service values?

2   Have other organisations received training from this trainer? Request confidential evaluations from those who were directly involved.

3   Does the trainer teach preventative strategies such as social interaction skills – calming techniques, coping strategies and developing positive behaviours?

4   Does the trainer emphasise the importance of reducing the use of restrictive physical interventions?

continued

5   Does the trainer teach concepts such as 'least restrictive intervention' and 'gradient of support'?

6   Does the trainer teach any techniques that cause pain or place pressure on joints?

7   Does the trainer emphasise the importance of refresher courses?

8   Can you attend a workshop given by the trainer before you engage them to train your staff? (If this is not possible, proceed with caution.) When attending a preview workshop do you consider whether the approach is consistent with the principles set out in this book? Do you consider whether staff are gaining confidence in their ability to use restrictive physical interventions with people who challenge? Is the training appropriate for the needs of your staff team?

9   Is the trainer willing to incorporate existing organisational policies into the training programme?

10 Does the trainer have a relevant professional qualification and experience (eg teacher, nurse, psychologist)? Does the trainer have a first-aid qualification?

Information on the BILD Accreditation Scheme (for those who offer training in the use of restrictive physical interventions) and the BILD Code of Practice (which provides guidance on commissioning training on restrictive physical interventions) can be found in the reference section.

Training in the use of restrictive physical interventions is not a one-off event. Services should aim to use restrictive physical interventions as little as possible. Paradoxically, in successful services staff may have relatively little opportunity to use restrictive physical interventions in real-life settings. In these circumstances, competencies will gradually diminish over time because they are not being used on a regular basis. All staff need to be kept up to date and have their skills reviewed by an experienced practitioner. It is important for all staff to have regular refresher courses in the use of restrictive physical interventions.

Good practice

Ashley Grove residential unit has one senior member of staff who trains and supports members of staff who use restrictive physical interventions. This member of staff regularly attends external courses. Ways of applying restrictive physical interventions are discussed by a multidisciplinary team so that all members of staff are familiar with the guidelines and recording procedures. The staff trainer is available to give practical advice and support to members of staff working with service users who present challenging behaviours.

Poor practice

Jimmy attends Spencer Park Day Service and often presents challenging behaviours. Following attendance on a one-day training course on control and restraint, the three biggest members of staff are expected to intervene whenever Jimmy gets 'out of order'.

Key policy principle 31   Staff should only use restrictive physical interventions that they have been taught by approved trainers.

There are many different types of restrictive physical intervention. Most training courses will only include a small number of the possible methods of using restrictive physical intervention. It is important that staff only use the specific methods covered in their training courses. Staff and service users may be placed at risk if staff use interventions for which they have not been trained.

Where staff have received different types of training, they will need clear guidance on the most appropriate forms of intervention. When working with any individual service user, all staff should use the same approach or method. All members of staff who work with a service user who may require restrictive physical interventions should be capable of using approved methods.

Good practice

Hightop House has a new resident who occasionally becomes extremely violent. While the staff team is developing a range of preventative and proactive strategies to help him, all staff have been taught a simple and safe form of restrictive physical intervention. No other 'hands on' methods of responding to aggressive outbursts are permitted.

 Poor practice

In Green Meadow School, there are a number of pupils who present severe challenging behaviours. Some staff have been on a course and have learned methods of 'passive restraint'. They have passed these on to their colleagues. The educational psychologist has recommended wrapping a duvet around children who are aggressive but has not been able to give any practical instruction on how this should be done. As a result, a variety of restrictive physical interventions are used by people with different levels of training.

Deploying appropriately trained staff

When levels of training and expertise vary across individual members of staff, special arrangements may be needed to ensure that any incident of challenging behaviour can be properly managed. This may include organising duty rotas so that members of staff who have been trained to use restrictive physical interventions are always available to work with particular service users.

Key policy principle 32 Staff deployment should be organised to ensure that appropriately trained staff are available to respond to any incident that requires restrictive physical intervention.

Good practice

Sunnyside Homes has a policy which states that all staff who work with service users who present violent or aggressive behaviour must receive regular training on restrictive physical interventions. Home managers have a training budget and are responsible for implementing the policy.

 Poor practice

Seaview House is a large residential unit for people who present a variety of challenging behaviours. The staff frequently use restrictive physical interventions. Because of long-term difficulties in recruiting and retaining staff, there is extensive use of agency staff and untrained staff on short-term contracts. Consequently, it has proved impossible to provide 24-hour cover with staff who have been trained to use restrictive physical interventions.

Agenda for action

1. Does your organisation provide a programme of training for staff who work with service users who present challenging behaviours?

2. Do the trainers who provide training have appropriate experience and qualifications?

3. How are the staff told about who can (and who cannot) use restrictive physical interventions with service users?

4. What are the arrangements to ensure that staff with appropriate experience and training are available to respond to incidents of challenging behaviour?

Appendix 1

Summary of key policy principles on restrictive physical interventions

The law and restrictive physical interventions

Key policy principle 1
Any restrictive physical intervention should be consistent with the legal obligations and responsibilities of care agencies and their staff and the rights and protection afforded to people with learning disabilities under the law.

Key policy principle 2
Working within the 'legal framework', services are responsible for the provision of care, including restrictive physical interventions, which are in the person's best interests.

A common values base

Key policy principle 3
Restrictive physical interventions should only be used in the best interests of the service user.

Key policy principle 4
Service users should be treated fairly and with courtesy and respect.

Key policy principle 5
Service users should be helped to make choices and be involved in making decisions that affect their lives.

Key policy principle 6
There should be experiences and opportunities for learning that are appropriate to the person's interests and abilities.

Prevention of violence and aggression

Key policy principle 7
Challenging behaviours can often be prevented by careful management of the setting conditions.

Key policy principle 8
The interaction between environmental setting conditions and personal setting conditions should be explored for each service user who presents a challenge and setting conditions should be modified to reduce the likelihood of challenging behaviours occurring.

Key policy principle 9
Secondary prevention procedures should be established to ensure that problematic episodes are supported appropriately with non-physical interventions before service users become violent or aggressive.

Key policy principle 10
For each service user who presents a challenge there should be individualised strategies for responding to incidents of violence and aggression that, where appropriate, should include directions for using restrictive physical interventions.

Promoting the best interests of service users

Key policy principle 11
Individualised procedures should be established to enable care staff to respond effectively to service users who are likely to present violent or reckless behaviour while ensuring the safety of all concerned.

Key policy principle 12
Restrictive physical interventions should only be used in conjunction with other strategies designed to help service users learn alternative non-challenging behaviours.

Key policy principle 13
Planned restrictive physical interventions should be justified in respect of what is known of the service user from a formal multidisciplinary assessment, alternative approaches that have been tried, an evaluation of the potential risks involved and references to a body of expert knowledge and established good practice.

Key policy principle 14
The use of restrictive physical interventions should be subject to regular review.

Restrictive physical interventions and risk assessment

Key policy principle 15
Physical interventions should not involve unreasonable risk and potential hazards associated with the use of restrictive physical interventions should be systematically explored using a risk assessment procedure.

Minimising risks and promoting the well-being of service users

Key policy principle 16
Restrictive physical interventions should be used with the minimum of reasonable force.

Key policy principle 17
Any single application of restrictive physical intervention should be used for the minimum period of time consistent with the best interests of the service user.

Key policy principle 18
The use of restrictive physical interventions should be sanctioned for the shortest period of time consistent with the individual service user's best interests.

Key policy principle 19
Restrictive physical interventions should not cause pain.

Key policy principle 20
Service users should have individual assessments to identify contraindications to restrictive physical interventions before they are approved.

Key policy principle 21
Service users who received a restrictive physical intervention should be routinely assessed for signs of injury or psychological distress.

Management responsibilities

Key policy principle 22
Service managers are responsible for developing and implementing policies on the use of restrictive physical interventions.

Key policy principle 23
The use of any restrictive physical intervention should be clearly set out in the form of written guidance for staff.

Key policy principle 24
Service managers are responsible for ensuring that all incidents that involve the use of a restrictive physical intervention are clearly, comprehensively and promptly recorded.

Key policy principle 25
All service users and their families and representatives should have ready access to an effective complaints system.

Key policy principle 26
Careful consideration should be given to the impact of resource management on the use of restrictive physical interventions.

Employers' responsibilities to staff

Key policy principle 27
Employers and managers are responsible for the safety and well-being of staff.

Key policy principle 28
All restrictive physical interventions and any associated incidents that give cause for concern must be recorded and reported.

Staff training

Key policy principle 29
Staff who may be required to use restrictive physical interventions should receive regular training on knowledge, skills and values.

Key policy principle 30
Training should be provided by a trainer with appropriate experience and qualifications.

Key policy principle 31
Staff should only use restrictive physical interventions that they have been taught by approved trainers.

Key policy principle 32
Staff deployment should be organised to ensure that appropriately trained staff are available to respond to any incident that requires restrictive physical intervention.

Appendix 2
Summary of agendas for action

The law and restrictive physical interventions

1. Does your service sanction the use of restrictive physical interventions for adults and/or children? If so, can you provide a justification in respect of both the criminal law and the civil law?

2. Is your use of restrictive physical interventions consistent with good practice as set out in guidance and circulars by government departments and regulatory bodies?

3. Are procedures in place to ensure that restrictive physical interventions are always used in the best interests of each individual service user?

A common values base

1. Are you clear about how the restrictive physical intervention helps the person concerned, ie is it used in their best interests?

2. Are there any conflicts of interest where you or members of staff experience fewer demands or less stress when the restrictive physical intervention is used?

3. Are the service users who experience restrictive physical interventions consulted before they are used?

4. What steps have been taken to ensure that the restrictive physical interventions minimise any loss of dignity for those concerned?

5. How far and in what ways do the restrictive physical interventions you employ reduce the person's opportunities for choice and making decisions?

6. What steps have been taken to reduce the likelihood that restrictive physical interventions will be needed in future?

7. What has been done to ensure that the use of restrictive physical interventions is combined with opportunities for new experiences and opportunities for learning?

Prevention of violence and aggression

1.   Which service users are likely to present violent or reckless behaviour?

2.   For each service user:

     ● What are the environmental setting conditions?

     ● What are the personal setting conditions?

     ● What are the triggers for violence and aggression?

3.   What primary prevention measures have been taken for each service user?

4.   What secondary prevention measures have been taken for each service user?

5.   Are there planned strategies for responding to the severe challenging behaviours that do occur?

Promoting the best interests of service users

1.   Are staff provided with written guidance on the permissible methods of restrictive physical intervention to be used with each service user?

2.   For each service user who may experience some form of restrictive physical intervention, what strategies are in place to promote alternative, more appropriate forms of communication and behaviour?

3.   Are restrictive physical interventions clearly justified in terms of the service user's previous history (including the range of alternative strategies that have been tried) and an up-to-date multidisciplinary assessment?

4.   Is there a written summary of the reasons for using a particular restrictive physical intervention with each service user?

5.   Do all service users who experience restrictive physical interventions receive regular routine reviews?

6.   Are the results of sensory assessments used to inform discussions about the most appropriate way of responding to challenging behaviour?

7.   Can additional reviews be triggered by changing circumstances surrounding the use of restrictive physical interventions?

Restrictive physical interventions and risk assessment

1.   What restrictive physical interventions are currently used or are sanctioned for use by members of staff?

2.   What are the potential hazards associated with using each procedure?

3.   Who is at risk when each restrictive physical intervention is used:

     ● the service user who needs the intervention?

     ● staff using the intervention?

     ● other service users and members of staff?

     ● members of the public?

4. What steps have been taken to minimise the likelihood that restrictive physical interventions will have adverse consequences for service users, staff and members of the public?

5. What is the least restrictive physical intervention that will enable staff to respond effectively to foreseeable incidents involving individual service users?

Minimising risks and promoting the well-being of service users

1. What steps have been taken to ensure that all instances of restrictive physical intervention are employed with the minimum of reasonable force?

2. How are restrictive physical interventions monitored to ensure that any single intervention is applied for the shortest period of time consistent with the service user's best interest?

3. How often are service users who receive restrictive physical interventions reviewed and what procedures are in place to ensure that alternative approaches (that do not involve restrictive physical interventions) are thoroughly explored?

4. What steps have been taken to ensure that the restrictive physical interventions used do not cause pain?

5. What steps have been taken to assess or reassess potential hazards and manage risk?

6. How are service users assessed for possible contraindications before restrictive physical interventions are approved?

7. Are service users who are exposed to restrictive physical interventions routinely assessed for signs of distress immediately following an incident and what steps are taken if there is evidence of distress or injury?

Management responsibilities

1. Is there a policy to guide you and any staff for whom you are responsible in the use of restrictive physical interventions?

2. Are you and any staff for whom you are responsible fully conversant with the contents of the policy relating to the use of restrictive physical interventions?

3. Have staff and service users, parents and advocates, been consulted on the contents of the policy?

4. Have other organisations that share responsibility for providing services for people who challenge been consulted?

5. Are there written guidelines for practice that describe the use of specific restrictive physical interventions with individual service users and are fully consistent with the policy relating to the use of restrictive physical interventions?

6. What methods are used to record the use of restrictive physical interventions? How is this information used to improve practice?

7. How do service users, their families and representatives use the complaints procedure?

8. How does the management of resources within the organisation affect the use of restrictive physical interventions and how can it be improved?

Employers' responsibilities to staff

1. Is the employer's responsibility for staff safety and well-being described in the policy document?

2. What are staff entitlements in the event of injury or psychological distress arising from the use of restrictive physical interventions?

3. How are staff encouraged to monitor good practice and report incidents that involve poor practice?

Staff training

1. Does your organisation provide a programme of training for staff who work with service users who present challenging behaviours?

2. Do the trainers who provide training have appropriate experience and qualifications?

3. How are the staff told about who can (and who cannot) use restrictive physical interventions with service users?

4. What are the arrangements to ensure that staff with appropriate experience and training are available to respond to incidents of challenging behaviour?

References

Ashton, G R and Ward, A D (1992) *Mental Handicap and the Law* London: Sweet and Maxwell

Association of Directors of Social Services (2005) *Safeguarding Adults: A National Framework of Standards for Good Practice and Outcomes in Adult Protection Work* London: Association of Directors of Social Services

Blunden, R (1988) Quality of life in persons with disabilities: issues in the development of services. In R I Brown (ed) *Quality of Life for Handicapped People* Beckenham: Croom Helm

Blunden, R and Allen, D (1987) *Facing the Challenge: An Ordinary Life for People with Learning Difficulties and Challenging Behaviour* London: King's Fund Centre

Brazier, M (1993) *The Law of Torts* London: Butterworths

British Institute of Learning Disabilities (2006) *BILD Code of Practice for the Use of Physical Interventions: A Guide for Trainers and Commissioners of Training* (2nd edition) Kidderminster: BILD

Clements, J (1996) Review of C M Lyon Issues Arising from the Care, Control and Safety of Children with Learning Disabilities who also Present Severe Challenging Behaviour. London: The Mental Health Foundation, *Journal of Applied Research in Intellectual Disability*, 9, 1, 80–82

Commission for Social Care Inspection (2005) on behalf of the Joint Inspectorate Steering Group *Safeguarding Children: The Second Joint Chief Inspectors' Report on Arrangements to Safeguard Children*

Davidson, J, McCullough, D, Steckley, L and Warren, T (eds) (2005) *Holding Safely: A Guide for Residential Child Care Practitioners and Managers about Physically Restraining Children and Young People* Glasgow: The Scottish Institute for Residential Child Care

Department of Health and Department for Education and Skills (2002) *Guidance on Restrictive Physical Interventions for People with Learning Disability and Autistic Spectrum Disorder in Health, Education and Social Care Settings* www.dh.gov.uk/assetRoot/04/06/84/61/04068461.pdf

Department of Health (1995) *The Health of the Nation: A Strategy for People with Learning Disabilities* London: HMSO

Department of Health and Home Office (2000) *No Secrets: Guidance on Developing and Implementing Multi-agency Policies and Procedures to Protect Vulnerable Adults from Abuse* London: Department of Health

Department of Health (2001) *Valuing People: A New Strategy for Learning Disability for the 21st Century*, London: HMSO

Department of Health/Welsh Office (1993) *Mental Health Act, 1983, Code of Practice* London: HMSO

Dimond, B (1995) *Legal Aspects of Nursing* London: Prentice Hall

Donnellan, A, Lavigna, G W, Negri-Shoultz, N and Fassbender, L L (1988) *Progress Without Punishment: Effective Approaches for Learners with Behavior Problems* New York: Teachers College Press

Doyle, A, Dunn, C, Allen, D and Hadley, J (1996) *Preventing and Responding to Aggressive Behaviour: A Training Manual* Cardiff: Welsh Centre for Learning Disabilities/Cardiff Community Healthcare

Emerson, E (1995) *Challenging Behaviour: Analysis and Intervention in People with Learning Disabilities* Cambridge: Cambridge University Press

Emerson, E, Barrett, S, Bell, C, Cummings, R, Hughes, H, McCool, C, Toogood, A and Mansell, J (1987) *The Special Development Team: Developing Services for People with Severe Learning Difficulties and Challenging Behaviours* Canterbury: University of Kent, Institute of Social and Applied Psychology

Harris, J (1996) Physical restraint procedures for managing challenging behaviours presented by mentally retarded adults and children, *Research in Developmental Disabilities*, 17, 2, 99–134

Harris, J C (2004) New guidance on the use of restrictive physical interventions *Tizard Learning Disability Review* 9, 2

Harris, P and Russell, O (1989) *The Nature of Aggressive Behaviour Among People with Learning Difficulties (Mental Handicap) in a Single Health District* Bristol: Norah Fry Research Centre

Health and Safety Executive (1989) *Violence To Staff* London: HMSO

Health and Safety Executive (1994) *Essentials of Health and Safety at Work* Sudbury: HSE Books

Hill, J and Spreat, S (1987) Staff injury rates associated with the implementation of contingent restraint, *Mental Retardation*, 25, 3, 141–145

Lyon, C M (1994a) *Legal Issues Arising from the Care, Control and Safety of Children with Learning Disabilities who also Present Challenging Behaviour* London: The Mental Health Foundation

Lyon, C M (1994b) *Legal Issues Arising from the Care and Control of Children with Learning Disabilities who also Present Severe Challenging Behaviour: A Guide for Parents and Carers* London: The Mental Health Foundation

Lyon, C M and Pimor, A (2004) *Physical Interventions and the Law: Legal Issues Arising from the Use of Physical Interventions in Supporting Children, Young People and Adults with Learning Disabilities and Severe Challenging Behaviour* Kidderminster: BILD

Martin, A E (ed) (2002) *Oxford Dictionary of Law* Oxford: Oxford University Press

McDonnell, A, Deardon, R and Richens, A (1991) Staff training in the management of violence and aggression, *Mental Handicap*, 19, 4, 151–154

McDonnell, A, Sturmey, P and Deardon, R (1993) The acceptability of physical restraint procedures for people with learning difficulty, *Behavioural and Cognitive Psychotherapy*, 21, 3, 255–264

Mental Welfare Commission for Scotland (June 2006) *Rights, Risks and Limits to Freedom: Principles and Good Practice Guidance for Practitioners Considering Restraint in Residential Care Settings*

Mental Welfare Commission for Scotland (November 2002) *Principles and Guidance on Good Practice in Caring for Residents with Dementia and Related Disorders and Residents with Learning Disabilities where Consideration is Being Given to the Use of Physical Restraint and Other Limits to Freedom*

Murphy, G, Kelly-Pike, A, McGill, P, Jones, S and Byatt, J (2003) Physical interventions with people with intellectual disabilities: staff training and policy frameworks *Journal of Applied Research in Intellectual Disabilities*, 16, 115–125

New York Office of Mental Retardation and Developmental Disabilities (1988) *Strategies for Crisis Intervention and Prevention: Instructor's Guide* Albany, New York: Office of Work Force Planning and Development

New York State Office of Mental Retardation and Developmental Disabilities (1997) *Strategies for Crisis Intervention and Prevention* (revised) SCIPr, Albany, New York

O'Brien, J (1987) A guide to lifestyle planning. In Wilcox B W and Bellamy G T *The Activities Catalogue: An Alternative Curriculum for Youth and Adults with Severe Disabilities* Baltimore: Paul H. Brookes

Perry, J and Felce, D (1995) Measure for measure: how do measures of quality of life compare? *British Journal of Learning Disabilities*, 23, 4, 134–137

Richardson, P J, Thomas, D A, Turner J, Shay, S and Carter, W (2003) *Archbold: Criminal Pleading, Evidence and Practice* London: Sweet & Maxwell

Rowett, C and Breakwell, G (1992) *Managing Violence at Work* Windsor: NFER-Nelson

Scottish Executive (2005) *Safe and Well: Good Practice in Schools and Education Authorities for Keeping Children Safe and Well*

Scottish Executive (2001) *The Same as You: A Review of Services for People with Learning Disabilities*

Scottish Executive Health Department letter signed by Geoff Huggins Head of Mental Health Division sent to relevant Chief Executives (dated 17 December 2004) *Safe Care – Consideration of the Recommendations from the Inquiry (England) into the Death of David Bennett*

Spreat, S, Lipinski, D P, Hill, J and Halpin, M (1986) Safety indices associated with the use of contingent restraint procedures, *Applied Research in Mental Retardation*, 7, 475–481

Welsh Assembly Government (2001) *Fulfilling the Promises*

Welsh Health Planning Forum (1992) *Protocol for Investment in Healthcare: Mental Handicap (Learning Disability)* Cardiff: Welsh Office NHS Directorate/Welsh Health Planning Forum

Willis, T J and Lavigna, G W (1985) *Emergency Management Guidelines* Los Angeles: IABA

BILD Physical Interventions Accreditation Scheme

The BILD Physical Interventions Accreditation Scheme (PIAS) is a nationally recognised accreditation scheme designed to help those responsible for commissioning training in the use of restrictive physical interventions to find providers who will deliver high-quality training based on the principles set out in this book.

The Scheme was developed in consultation with commissioners of training, instructors in physical interventions, service users, professional organisations and government bodies to address a need for accreditation of training and instruction in the management of violence and aggression which includes de-escalation strategies as well as physical intervention techniques.

The Scheme was funded by the Department of Health (DoH) and the Department for Education and Skills (DfES) with the aim of providing a clear set of criteria for assessing the training provided for staff who support children and adults with learning disabilities or autistic spectrum disorder. DoH/DfES *Guidance on Restrictive Physical Interventions for People with Learning Disability and Autistic Spectrum Disorder in Health, Education and Social Care Settings* (2002) recognises the need for all staff to be trained in the use of restrictive physical interventions and for trainers to be carefully selected.

The benefits of accreditation include:

- The *Code of Practice for the Use of Physical Interventions* (2006) provides an important set of standards about training in the use of physical interventions for trainers and service providers.
- Employers and managers have information to inform their decisions in the use of particular training.
- It enables training organisations to provide information on the quality of training they provide.

The Scheme is suitable for organisations that provide training for staff working with children and adults who are described as having:

- learning disabilities/difficulties
- autistic spectrum disorders
- emotional and behavioural difficulties
- special educational needs (in particular those with learning disabilities and autistic spectrum disorder)

To be eligible to apply for accreditation, training organisations must have formally adopted the BILD Code of Practice. Organisations that are successful in applying to the BILD PIAS will have accredited status for a period of three years and will be included in the BILD Physical Interventions Accreditation Database (PIAD) of training organisations/ instructors. Details of all accredited organisations will also appear on the BILD website.